Praise for Saving

"*Saving Public Education,* provides a powerful launchpad for setting public education on a path for great success. The author's thoughts and ideas spring from his 20 years of service in the Texas Legislature; countless years as a businessman in Aerospace, Manufacturing, Banking, and Real Estate; and most of all, many years of meaningful citizenship advocacy on behalf of high-quality public education. **For those interested in better public schooling outcomes, this is a must-read."**
—**Dr. Rod Page**, former U.S. Secretary of Education

"This book has caused me to reconsider most of the ideals I have had regarding public education. **The opportunity for teachers to own their careers is the factor that I think has the most potential.** Teachers can do this."
—**Doug Rogers**, retired Executive Director of largest teacher organization in Texas

"Having started my 25-year public policy career with Kent Grusendorf, I can confidently say that he has given deeper thought to public education, its problems, and how to solve them, than the vast majority of those who work in the system on a daily basis. **His idea to actively put teachers, the real education practitioners, in full charge of their students' educations is the breath of fresh air education reform efforts have needed for decades."**
—**Dr. Byron Schlomach**, Chief Economist, 1889 Institute

"I finished reading *Saving Public Education.* I like it a lot! It is very well written, follows a logical flow of development, and makes the essential points for the need for public education reform **and, most importantly, puts forward a plan that, unlike what has gone before, puts the power back where it belongs**: with parents and teachers."
—**Dr. Don McAdams**, professor emeritus, author, consultant, and school board member

"Kent Grusendorf's entrepreneurial experiences and passion for education are melded together into this excellent summary of how America has failed our students and, most importantly, what should be done now. **Discussions about how to improve our public education system have been circular for decades.** Through his research and experiences, Kent Grusendorf has astutely identified a solution—**respect and reward the professionalism of our teachers."**
—**Linda Pavlik**, journalism professional and advocate for children

"No one is more qualified to identify the current deficiencies of public education and recommend strategies to address them than Kent Grusendorf. He has spent much of his professional life in this pursuit as a ten term member of the Texas House of Representatives, including four years as Chairman of its Public Education Committee. His book reflects thoughtful reflection on this legacy, outlines a bold transformational response to the challenge we face in delivering quality public education to our children and our future, and restores the classroom teacher to the primary leadership role in this transformation. **It deserves wide dissemination among education opinion leaders.**"

—**Jim Windham,** former banker, founder of Texas Institute for Education Reform, and reform activist

"Kent, in his book *Saving Public Education,* reveals the urgency to change attitudes. Attitudes toward teachers and education administrators. **Teachers are not THE problem to fix**, they are people to be respected, guided, empowered and trained in innovating solutions for our student's sake."

—**Steve Swanson**, professional engineer and school reform advocate

"Anybody who thinks the educational models of yesteryear work today ... don't understand the current degradation happening in public schools. The statistics and the explanations in this book prove we need revolutionary new models. Read about his description of the 'Professional Teacher Act.' **I say it is the 'butterfly' among the 'caterpillars' in today's failed attempts at school reform.**"

—**Dr. Kenneth Poppee**, former ATPE Teacher of the Year

"This book is very enlightening, and **I believe everyone in the education system would benefit from reading** it as it explains a tremendous amount about the history and evolution of our education system. It also suggests innovative ideas for the future of the education system. As teachers, we should always be receptive to ideas which will benefit our students and our profession."

—**Melissa Martin**, high school teacher and member of the Texas Juvenile Justice Board.

Saving Public Education
Setting Teachers Free to Teach

Kent Grusendorf

Copyright © Kent Grusendorf 2020

All rights reserved.

ISBN: 978-1-945028-30-4

Published by Texans for Real Efficiency and Equity in Education

Colored pencils photo (4) by Agence Olloweb on Unsplash
Window photo (7) by Clark Young on Unsplash
Teacher illustration (8) licensed from Shutterstock
Photo of Virginia City schoolroom (9) by author
One-Room Schoolhouse photo (10) by David Gylland on Unsplash
School Building photo (13) by Aaron Burden on Unsplash
Notebooks photo (21) by John Mark Smith on Unsplash
Protest photo (58) by Bob Blob on Unsplash
Bike and barn photo (59) is from Pixnio
Strike photo (69) by LaTerrian McIntosh on Unsplash
Hot Air Balloon (80) photo by ian dooley on Unsplash
Football stadium (96) photo from Pogue Construction
Pen and Paper photo (105) by Aaron Burden on Unsplash
Texas governor photos (111-118) from the public domain
Child reading photo (127) by Aaron Burden on Unsplash
Old phone photo (133) by Quina Al on Unsplash
Desk with Inkwell photo (152) by Pexels on Pixabay

> "We're living in the 21st century while insisting on an education architecture built for the 1800s… It's time to construct an entirely new system."
>
> —Texas Governor Greg Abbott, 2017 *State of the State Address*

Contents

ix	Preface
3	Introduction
7	Chapter 1 *The Teacher*
17	Chapter 2 *Administrative Control*
31	Chapter 3 *A System at Risk*
65	Chapter 4 *Merit Pay—A Fool's Errand*
71	Chapter 5 *Teacher Pay*
75	Chapter 6 *Teachers as True Professionals: The Professional Teacher Act, A New/Old Concept*
91	Chapter 7 *Money Matters: How Money Flows is Critical*
103	Chapter 8 *Education Reform*
125	Chapter 9 *The Achievement Gap Can Be Closed*
137	Chapter 10 *Equity, Adequacy, & Litigation*
145	Chapter 11 *Original Intent of the Texas Constitution*
157	Chapter 12 *Are We Funding Our Own Demise Through Higher Education?*

PREFACE

Saving Public Education: Setting Teachers Free to Teach

This book explores a potentially new professional opportunity for teachers. **Most teachers are in the profession because they love to teach.** However, far too many leave the profession due to lack of respect, excessive external pressures, and general frustration. Many teachers stay in the profession, but yearn for greater freedom to just do what the love: Teach. Much of that frustration comes from mandates, and a lack of professional freedom.

Well intentioned education reform advocates have attempted to reform the American education system for more than half a century. Most of these reform efforts have been designed in a way that imposes top-down mandates on our schools and teachers.

However, half a century later, despite much hard work by educators, the minority achievement gap remains at unacceptable levels. According to the Brookings Institute, no progress has been made in literacy since NAEP testing began in 1971; poor students perform three or four years behind grade level; and far too many teachers are frustrated with a system that fails to treat them as true professionals.

A better solution would have been to free teachers to teach.

Virtually all meaningful reform efforts over the past few decades have either failed to produce the desired results, or have been undone over time due to political pressure. **It is time** to acknowledge one simple fact: **Top-down reform efforts, and mandates on teachers, have not worked and will not work, as intended.**

Over the past three decades, teacher pay, after adjusting for inflation, has decreased. This has occurred despite the fact that spending, also adjusted for inflation, has increased dramatically. Today, Americans spend about $4 billion per school day on public education. Annually, we spend about $350,000 per classroom of 25; however, we only pay teachers about $60,000.

Over the past seven decades administrative staff has increased by over 750%. That is indicative of a system which simply has its priorities wrong.

America's political leaders need to understand that there is a subtle yet distinct difference between what is best for institutions and what is best for student success. **Unfortunately, in America today, school funding is based primarily on institutional needs rather than student and teacher needs.** Formulas are designed to fund the system rather than fund education within the system.

Today, teachers are paid less than their true market value, in part due to monopsony power, and often lack necessary classroom supplies. Teachers are the backbone of the system, yet many are frustrated, and they should be, by lack of professional recognition, and lack of adequate financial support for their classrooms.

In public education's early years teachers were actually in charge of the school; they answered directly to parents and taxpayers. Most importantly, they had the ability to do what they thought best for their students. **Today, teachers answer to multiple layers of school administrators, and to local, state, and**

federal politicians, all of whom impose top-down dictates upon these teachers and their schools.

It is time to acknowledge that top-down control has not worked well for millions of American students. The answer will not come from above. The answer is in the classrooms of America today. **The solution is to set teachers free to teach.**

Teachers are the individuals who actually deliver education services. The system should be organized accordingly. If organized correctly, educators would be set free from politics and be allowed to focus totally on educating children. **To accomplish that objective, teachers must be treated as real professionals, not just given lip service that they "are" professionals.**

Saving Public Education makes the case with simple data that the best way to reward teachers is to allow them to practice their trade as true professionals. Teachers would be empowered by allowing a new optional component to the education systems current structure.

This new option would be the professional teacher concept. The *Professional Teacher Act* would provide a new option for teachers –the freedom to practice as true professionals- that would be a win-win for the entire profession.

Once the money held in trust for students is allowed to follow the child and teacher, there is no limit to the creative initiatives teachers could implement to achieve superior results for their students, for the education system, and for society.

The professional teacher concept would be a new option only available to certain public school teachers. It would allow a public school teacher who has been rated as proficient, or better, for three years to enter into "private practice," much like a doctor, or lawyer, who is in private practice. Students would not be "assigned" to any teacher in private practice. If students choose a teacher in private practice, the state money would flow directly to the teacher.

This professional teacher concept is a win-win for the entire education profession, for children, and for society. Educators would be empowered to specialize and innovate to meet the individual needs of their individual students. Teacher pay would be enhanced as well, both for those who participate in the program and for those who remain in the current system. This is because the monopsony power, held by school districts, represses teacher pay to a level below market value. Setting teachers free to practice their trade would change that dynamic for the entire profession.

Bottom line: The purpose of such a new professional opportunity would be to give education professionals the opportunity to function independently, with property rights similar to those afforded other professionals and the rewards inherent in those rights. Further, to allow highly qualified education professionals the opportunity to innovate and create educational programs suited for the specific needs of their student clientele.

Saving Public Education
Setting Teachers Free to Teach

INTRODUCTION

> All who have meditated on the art of governing mankind have been convinced that **the fate of empires depends on the education of youth.**
>
> —Aristotle

As expressed by Aristotle in the 3rd century BC, nothing is more important to the future of a state or nation than the education of its children. Nothing is as important to a child's educational future as the teacher.

Public education as we know it today is working well for some students, and failing to work well for many others, such as students trapped in inner-city schools, students with special needs, and those who just fall through the cracks. But this is not the time for placing blame, nor a time to espouse excuses. Instead, it is time to focus on what can be done to benefit all the children of this great nation.

Public education—providing a general diffusion of knowledge to youth—is one of the most important things we do as a society. However, too often the system delivering that knowledge is the focus of political decisions rather than decisions focused on those receiving such services, or those who actually perform the service, teachers.

This book will review the critical role that classroom teachers play in public education. It will explore the historical role of the teacher, and the role of teachers, or lack thereof, in modern education reform efforts. It will also examine what might be considered a novel concept: Empowering classroom teachers to drive future education reform dynamics.

The book will also review the major education reform efforts over the past half-century and examine the long-term impact of past reform efforts on students and teachers. It will review major future political risks to public education and potential solutions. It will discuss the folly of top-down education reform efforts, including merit pay and other reforms, which have either produced little to no success, or when they have been successful, were reversed due to political pressures.

This book will explore new ideas as to how the problems and risks to the public education system might be resolved from within the system by setting teachers, and administrators, free to truly exercise their trade. It will briefly review some history of public education, including its original intent, its structure, and the ways it has been financed.

This book will explore how future reform efforts might allow teachers to play a major role in enhancing the public education system for the mutual benefit of its students, its teachers, and the public interest. It will explore creative change that would allow classroom teachers greater latitude to innovate, and would put teachers in greater control of educational decision-making. It will examine a new concept that would, instead of just giving teachers the lip service of being called professionals, actually allow classroom teachers to serve as professionals in the truest sense.

CHAPTER 1

The Teacher

What constitutes a school? One thing we know for sure: **A school absent the teacher is just an empty building.**

All evidence supports the fact that the most significant factor in quality education is the teacher. Although nothing matters more to the education of a child, today's public education system fails to adequately recognize and adequately reward classroom teachers for the critical role they play. And the system as organized greatly undervalues the main place where education occurs: The classroom. If our states and nation are to prosper, this must change.

The system greatly undervalues the main place where education occurs: The classroom.

As structured today, teachers work for the school system; teachers work for school administrators; they work for school boards; and they work as directed by congress and state legislators. Although in this hierarchy teachers are referred to as professionals, in reality they must practice their profession as directed by many others.

School administrators do not educate kids; instead, they function as support staff for the teaching that occurs primarily in the classroom. This support staff, if not excessive, is important in accomplishing the goal of delivering quality education to children. However, what occurs in the classroomw is significantly more important. At present, things are upside down.

In most professions, those professionals who are actually doing the critical work are in charge. In education, the professional teacher is usually subservient to many administrators. Although it is true that most school administrators are trained educators, the fact is most have been out of the classroom for a good while and are unfamiliar with the specific needs of the specific students whom the teacher sees every day. Without question, the practicing teacher has greater knowledge of the dynamics in the classroom on any given day, and has better information regarding what will motivate or inspire the students assigned to that class. Bottom line: The teacher is the actual practitioner. Yet, in our current system, they are subservient to many others.

The present system is akin to one in which attorneys work for their law firm's support staff, or doctors working for the administrators and technicians who support their medical services. Few attorneys would win at the courthouse in such a situation, practicing their trade based on decisions made by people unfamiliar with the specific characteristics and

needs of their clients or the circumstances surrounding their individual cases. Doctors would save fewer lives if they had to comply with the dictates of support staff who lack the knowledge of the practitioner who actually examined the patient. Regardless of whether educational support staff is made up of trained professionals or interns, their primary role should always be to support the work done in the classroom by the professional in charge of that classroom.

A truly efficient public education system would be different from what it is today. Those who actually deliver professional services, that is to say teachers, would be given a superior innovation and oversight role. Teachers would practice like doctors, lawyers, accountants, and other professionals. Considering the critical nature of their mission, these professionals would receive compensation more commensurate with other professionals. A manner to achieve these objectives can be found in Chapter 6 of this book

The One-Room Schoolhouse

The current top-down, assembly-line system for public education stands in stark contrast with educational history. Let us briefly examine the schoolhouse of a century ago.

In the one-room schoolhouse, the teacher was in total control. The entire community acknowledged the teacher as the professional in charge of educating its children. The teacher made virtually all education-related decisions at the schoolhouse. The teacher did not work from a script as determined by state, federal, and local administrators. Instead the teacher tailored the curriculum, and his or her teaching, to the needs of individual students. The students were typically of varying ages, so teaching required a focus on the individual rather than group learning.

Those 19th and early 20th century teachers did not have the resources available to teachers today. They had no Internet they could use to find curriculum ideas or other help. They had no supervisor they could go to with their problems. However, the one thing they did have was near total control over the school and their classrooms. There were no state mandates, and no federal mandates. Instead, teachers exercised common sense to run their schools.

Considering the challenges, those 19th century teachers did a great job. Some researchers contend that the eighth-grade curriculum in 1895 was equivalent to college level work today.[1] Take a look at the 1895 Eight Grade graduation test below to see the rigor teachers expected from their students:

---

[1] Josie Brady, "Education in the 1800's;" https://www.education.ne.gov/wp-content/uploads/2017/07/Education_in_the_1800s.pdf

8th Grade Test:
Kansas, Circa 1895

GRAMMAR [Time, one hour]

1. Give the nine rules for the use of Capital Letters.
2. Name the parts of speech and define those that have no modifications.
3. Define: Verse, Stanza and Paragraph.
4. What are the principal parts of a verb? Give the Principal Parts of do, lie, lay, and run.
5. What is Punctuation? Give rules for principal marks of punctuation.
6. Define Case. Illustrate each case.
7. Write a composition of about 150 words and show there in that you understand the practical use of the rules of grammar.

ARITHMETIC [Time, 1½ hours]

1. Name and define the Fundamental Rules of Arithmetic.
2. A wagon box is 2 ft. deep, 10 feet long, and 3 ft. wide. How many bushels of wheat will it hold?
3. If a load of wheat weighs 3,942 pounds, what is it worth at 50 cts. Per bu., deducting 1050 lbs. for tare?
4. District No. 33 has a valuation of $35,000. What is the necessary levy to carry on a school seven months at $50 per month, and have $104 for incidentals?
5. Find the cost of 6,720 lbs. coal at $6.00 per ton.
6. Find the interest of $512.60 for 8 months and 18 days at 7 per cent.
7. What is the cost of 40 boards 12 inches wide and 16 ft. long at $20 per in.?
8. Find bank discount on $300 for 90 days [no grace] at 10 per cent.
9. What is the cost of a square farm at $15 per acre, the distance around which is 640 rods?
10. Write a Bank check, a Promissory Note, and a Receipt.

U.S. HISTORY [Time, 45 minutes]

1. Give the epochs into which U.S. History is divided.
2. Give an account of the discovery of America by Columbus.
3. Relate the causes and results of the Revolutionary War.
4. Show the territorial growth of the United States.
5. Tell what you can of the history of Kansas.
6. Describe three of the most prominent battles of the Rebellion.

ORTHOGRAPHY [Time, 1½ hours]

1. What is meant by the following: Alphabet, Phonetic, Orthography, Etymology, Syllabication?
2. What are elementary sounds? How classified?
3. What are the following, and give examples of each: Trigraph, Subvocals, Diphthong, Cognate, Linguals?
4. Give two uses of silent letter in spelling. Illustrate each.
5. Define the following prefixes and use in connection with a word: Bi, Dis, Mis, Pre, Semi, Post, Non, Inter, Mono, Super.
6. Mark diacritically and divided into syllables the following, and name the sign that indicates the sound: Card, ball mercy, sir, odd, cell, rise, blood, fare, last.
7. Use the following correctly in sentences: Cite, site, sight, fane, fain, feign, vane, vein, raze, raise, rays. Write 10 words frequently mispronounced and indicate pronunciation by use of diacritical marks and by syllabication.[2]

---

2 **Test Source:** "Education in the 1800's," Josie Brady; https://www.education.ne.gov/wp-content/uploads/2017/07/Education_in_the_1800s.pdf

Before the explosion of administrative growth and oversight, teaching was more rewarding. True, teaching in a one-room schoolhouse was a very tough job, but it also provided great job satisfaction, greater professionalism, and surprisingly better comparative compensation. Education funding at that time was focused almost totally on the teacher. There was virtually no administrative overhead so almost 100% of education funding went directly to the teacher.

Typically, school facilities were provided by entities such as a local church, masonic lodge, another non-profit entity, or the community itself. Today, if education funding went only to teachers, aside from facilities funding, then teacher pay would be about $250,000.00 annually. However, the average teacher gets only about $60,000[3] and the rest of non-facilities funding goes to school administrators and administrative overhead. (See Chapters 4 and 5 for a discussion of teacher compensation.)

Things changed from the teacher/student-centered system of the 19th century. According to one education professor, there was a "struggle for control of American education in the early twentieth century between two factions of the movement for progressive education. The administrative progressives won this struggle, and they reconstructed the organization and curriculum of American schools in a form that has lasted to

---

3   *U.S. News and World Report*; https://money.usnews.com/careers/best-jobs/high-school-teacher/salary

the present day. Meanwhile the other group, the pedagogical progressives…failed miserably in shaping what we do in schools…."[4]

This professor argues that the losing side in this debate, the pedagogical progressives, would have instead molded 20th century public education very differently from the highly structured system of curriculum delivery and testing regiments we see in America today. If the other faction had prevailed, he asserts the system would focus on "…teaching students the skills they need in order to learn any subject, instead of focusing on transmitting a particular subject; it means promoting discovery and self-directed learning by the student through active engagement; it means having students work on projects that express student purposes and that integrate the disciplines around socially relevant themes; and it means promoting values of community, cooperation, tolerance, justice and democratic equality. In the shorthand of educational jargon, this adds up to 'child-centered instruction,' 'discovery learning' and 'learning how to learn.'"[5]

The professor may be right or wrong in his analysis of what might have been. However, one thing is certain: During the 20th century the American education system moved dramatically away from a teacher-driven, student-centered system to a top-down, administrative-heavy system focused on standardized group learning rather than individualized learning. Education in America moved away from the historical educational approaches used by some of the great teachers throughout history such as Socrates, Aristotle, and Plato.

---

4   David F. Labaree, Progressivism, Schools and Schools of Education: An American Romance, *Paedagogica Historica, Vol. 41, Nos. 1&2, pp. 275-288*
5   ibid

Education in America was therefore transformed from the historical education approaches used by some of the great teachers throughout history such as Socrates, Aristotle, and Plato.

Today, politicians and bureaucrats make the rules, whereas the great teachers of the past exercised discretion regarding the education of their students based on common sense, individual student needs, and classroom circumstances. **Too often today, rules and regulations trump the judgment of the classroom teacher**. That dynamic is a significant contrast from the one-room schoolhouse where parents picked the teacher and the teacher made the rules for the classroom.

In the late 1800s and early 1900s, education was also much more community oriented. In a small community there might be only one schoolhouse. In larger communities parents might choose from multiple schools and thus send their children to the teacher they preferred. The distinction between "public" and "private" schools did not exist at that time either. Instead, many states reimbursed both private and public schools for educating children.[6] In either instance, the teachers and parents were in charge. Politics did not drive education; instead, the objective and driving force was the education of individual children.

Over the decades, the system evolved into the highly structured, rules-driven, top-down system of today. Most likely animated by the Industrial Revolution, the system morphed

---

6   Billy Walker, Executive Director TASB, *Intent of the Framers in the Education Provisions of the Texas Constitution of 1876*, p.639; and Eby, *The Development of Education in Texas*, 1925

into something more akin to a production assembly line than a system which specialized in individual learning. Over time group learning became the norm. Individualized learning, as practiced by the educator in the one-room schoolhouse, and those before, became inconsistent with the rules-based system imposed by administrators and education experts from afar.

Today, as in the past, the teacher is both a vessel of knowledge and a facilitator for learning. Which is more important, that knowledge or the ability to enable and encourage learning? That is a question that can only be answered on an individual basis. The strengths of one teacher will differ from the strengths of another. Likewise, the needs of one student will differ from the needs of another student. The emotional dynamics of a classroom may also differ from one day to another, and from one hour to another.

Considering the fact that the classroom teacher is the one who actually delivers public education, the system is obviously structured in a manner that fails to allocate resources effectively to maximize the importance of that reality. **As organized, the system fails to adequately empower teachers with the opportunity to fully exploit their individual talents by assuming they should all teach the same curricula in similar "best practices" manners.**

Meaningful education reform will require allowing teachers to practice as genuine professionals. See Chapter 6 for an idea to actually implement that vision.

CHAPTER 2

Administrative Control—
The Teacher is Not in Charge Today

> What's wrong with education cannot be fixed with technology. The problem is bureaucracy.
>
> —Steve Jobs

Politicians, bureaucrats, and school administrators control education today. They determine the testing regiment, they determine curricula standards, they determine reporting requirements, they mandate education policy, and they write the rules. Teachers serve at their pleasure.

Today's top-down education system treats teachers more like hourly assembly-line workers than like true professionals. Instead of being allowed to function as independent professionals they work for school administrators and for politicians.

Most teachers' first loyalty is to their students. However, since teachers work directly for school administrators, if a teacher wishes to remain in the system and also move up the professional career ladder, a teacher must go into school administration. By leaving the classroom and moving to a support role, they are able to embellish their pay, gain greater professional recognition, and obtain greater status within the system.

Unfortunately, the incentive is to cease teaching students in order to become a member of administrative staff.

That's right: Unfortunately, **the professional incentive is to cease teaching students in order to become a member of administrative staff.** Today, around the country, non-teaching staff exceeds teaching staff.[7] Less than 50% of school staff play productive roles in the classroom.

School administrative staff in America has increased 758% in 67 years.
[see chart below]

School administration is important; support staff is important. However, **the system definitely has its priorities wrong.** A great teacher leaving the classroom for an administrative job is equivalent to a great surgeon leaving the operating room to oversee the blood-testing lab.

---

7   Mark J. Perry, "The staffing surge in America's public schools," March 7, 2013, American Enterprise Institute; http://www.aei.org/publication/the-staffing-surge-educratification-in-americas-public-schools-educrats-now-outnumber-teachers-in-25-states/print/

> Some years ago, the chairman of a legislative education committee received a phone call. The young man on the line told the chairman:
>
> "I need your help. Up until last year I served as a classroom teacher. I loved teaching; I was really good at teaching. However, I could no longer support my family on my teacher's pay so I moved into administration.
>
> "This year I'm serving as assistant principal. This job is important, but not nearly as important as my former job in the classroom.
>
> "I enjoyed teaching, and in reality, I was a better teacher than administrator. My superiors are happy with the job I'm doing and I probably have a good future in school administration.
>
> "However, I really miss the classroom; unfortunately, I had to move up in order to bring home the bacon for my family.
>
> "The system has its priorities wrong. Can you fix it?"

Non-teaching staff is only of value to the extent that their roles actually enhance the teacher's classroom efforts. Staff should support teachers, not tell them how and what to do. In this respect, the system has things upside down. Instead of staff working for the teachers, the teachers work for the staff.

Today, teachers are expected to merely insert knowledge, as determined by politicians and school administrators. They are expected to insert this knowledge as though students are passing through an assembly line at predetermined ages, instead of delivering that knowledge based upon their individual strengths, and needs of both themselves and their students.

Teachers are expected to do all this in accordance with rules established by politicians and school administrators.

It is difficult, if not impossible, to develop rules in a top-down system that adequately compensate for all individual circumstances and for all individual talents—the individual talents of students as well as the individual talents of teachers.

Yet, the system continues to exert an ever increasing control from above. As a result, the size of administrative staff has increased dramatically in America. In fact, in 2017, there were 150,000 more non-teachers on staff in America's public schools than teachers.[8] So, as of 2017, over half of all public school employees are non-teachers.

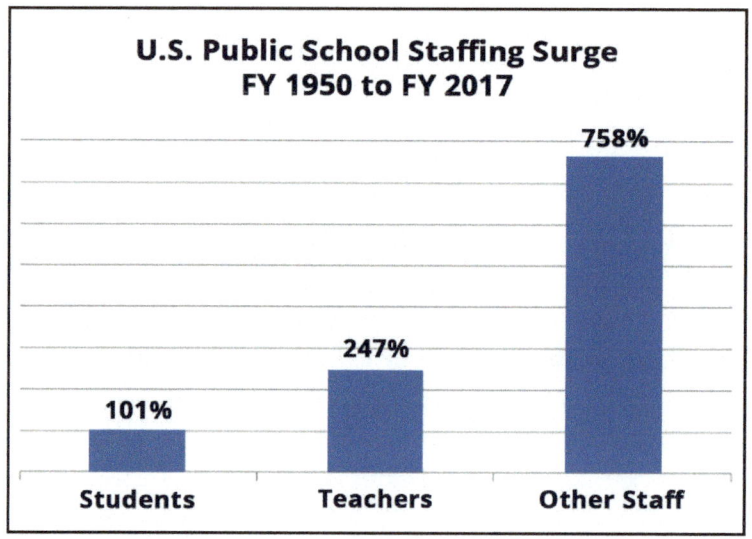

Chart courtesy of Ben Scafidi: PP Update (10/9/2019) to report found at: https://www.edchoice.org/wp-content/uploads/2017/06/Back-to-the-Staffing-Surge-by-Ben-Scafidi.pdf

---

8 https://www.cnsnews.com/news/article/zoey-dimauro/study-half-all-school-employees-not-teachers-130-increase-1970; also Dr. Benjamin Scafidi; https://www.edchoice.org/wp-content/uploads/2017/06/Back-to-the-Staffing-Surge-by-Ben-Scafidi.pdf

According to research by Dr. Benjamin Scafidi, although student enrollment grew by 101% between 1950 and 2017, **non-teacher staff grew by 758%.** If the non-teaching staff in American schools had increased at the same rate as student growth, the nation could have saved over $45 billion dollars in recurring annual savings. That could have added $14,340, on average, to the annual salary of every teacher in America.[9]

Although there is an obvious and necessary role for administrative support staff, the question is one of proper balance. What is the appropriate balance among teachers, support staff, and students? What is the cost-benefit of substituting resources to pay non-teaching staff instead of teachers? A proper balance of non-teaching staff who actually labor to support the efforts of teachers is totally appropriate. Excessive staff, however, which control and inhibit rather than function in a truly supportive role, generates gross inefficiencies throughout the entire public education system.

With this growth of support staff, it is natural for those in administrative positions to exercise more oversight and exert greater

---

9   Dr. Benjamin Scafidi, Power Point update (10/9/2019) to published report found at: https://www.edchoice.org/wp-content/uploads/2017/06/Back-to-the-Staffing-Surge-by-Ben-Scafidi.pdf

control. More staffers exercising oversight will inherently result in a growing rulebook. **A more efficient and productive model would be for administrative staff to exercise greater support for classroom teachers and less control over them.** That dynamic is determined by how the system is structured, and by which individual is in charge and which person is subservient.

I am supposedly doing what I love, but I don't recognize this profession as the one that I fell in love with in Finland.
– Kristiina Chartouni, a veteran Finnish educator who began teaching in an American high school

---

Many classroom teachers are justifiably frustrated with the degree of oversight and control, which can either allow them to be "productive or desperate and crushed."[10] Excessive oversight and control contributes to teacher frustration, suppression of innovation, and is costly to the entire system in terms of both human potential and money. Dr. Scafidi found that if non-teaching staff growth had only paralleled student enrollment growth, and if that money instead had gone to the classroom, then Texas teachers could have been paid an additional $19,424 per year, Virginia teachers about $30,000 more per year, and Mississippi teachers could have earned another $10,000 per year.[11]

This study only examined one aspect of excessive waste—the direct cost of hiring additional support staff. However, in

---

10   What Teachers Want You To Know–A Note to School Administrators, at https://www.cultofpedagogy.com/letter-to-administrators/
11   The School Staffing Surge, Decades of Employment Growth in America's Public Schools, Benjamin Scafidi, Ph.D., February 2013; https://files.eric.ed.gov/fulltext/ED543118.pdf

addition to this direct cost there is also an indirect cost—the inefficiencies inherent from excessive bureaucratic administrations and one-size-fits-all decision-making. This cost, although almost impossible to calculate, is assuredly many times larger than the direct cost of labor for the excess administrative staff, as calculated in the referenced report.

Many classroom teachers can relate to the following set of rules for intentionally growing a bureaucracy and creation of inefficiencies as outlined by a German engineer who grew up in East Germany when it was still part of the USSR:

> **"Rules for Growing a Bureaucracy**
>
> "Any organization needs rules. But instead of having a small and clear rule set, try to have a complex system with lots of special rules.
>
> "Never create any complete rules overview. Instead make up new rules all the time and let other people do the same. You've reached the ideal state of affairs when all people receive more than one new rule every week by email and there are so many special rules that people regularly break them and get reprimanded. This will make sure that people become very nervous about breaking a rule and think for a long time before doing anything out of the ordinary.
>
> "If you cannot think of more rules yourself, keep adopting the latest management fad. No matter how stupid it is and how stupid it sounds, subjugate your employees to sprints and daily scrums and heap the going literature on them, containing more rules, checklists, planning guides, and the like."[12]

12   Hans-Georg Michna, *In Search of Inefficiency,* How to Secure Jobs By Being Inefficient; http://michna.com/inefficiency.htm

A great deal of research indicates that education decisions made closer to the student produce superior results; however, unlike the past, the **public education system is almost entirely driven by politicians and bureaucrats who have little direct knowledge of what is needed in any specific classroom.** It bears repeating that school administrators do not educate children, politicians do not educate students, and, instead, students are educated at the campus level by classroom teachers. Yet, both politicians and administrators exercise significant control over what happens in today's schoolhouse. Therefore, rules rather than professional judgement have become the ultimate controlling factor.

Just as it is impossible to design an assembly line for custom-built homes, it is incomprehensible that politicians and bureaucrats could provide rules and regulations tailored to the individual needs of every child. Likewise, it is impossible to impose one teaching standard that works best for all teachers. Unfortunately, to an unacceptable extent, that is exactly what our current school system attempts to do. Rather than addressing the underlying problem, virtually every school reform effort over the past half-century has attempted to impose top-down solutions. See Chapter 8 for a discussion of various reform efforts and a list of fads tried over the years.

Overlooked is the reality that the real solution may be available within the system from within the teaching corps if we find a way to set teachers free. More on that concept in Chapter 6.

Politicians and bureaucrats also drive funding, and funding drives other decision-making. Since the middle of the 20th century, American education has experienced a significant change in funding methods. Those changes have led to school funding based on institutional needs as opposed to student/teacher needs. Today, both teachers and their students have become pawns in that funding system.

School funding formulas around the nation are based on institutional needs rather than student needs.

As indicated previously, with this change towards a totally top-down system, administrative growth exploded late in the 20th century and continues to grow exponentially in the 21st century. This is evidenced by the previously cited statistic that in only 67 years, non-teaching school staff in American schools increased by 758% while student enrollment grew by only 101%.[13]

This huge growth in administrative bloat has required significant additional funding for education, money which has not gone to teachers nor the classroom effort. Money is a critical necessity in education, but *how* that money is spent is even more important. As one education professor stated: "We spend millions on things that don't matter, and then we get jaundiced."[14] An eight-fold increase in administrative/support staffing is a prime example of growing administrative control, and of the very inefficient allocation of scarce resources.

---

13 Dr. Benjamin Scafidi, 2019 Power Point Presentation updating his 2017 data at: https://www.edchoice.org/wp-content/uploads/2017/06/Back-to-the-Staffing-Surge-by-Ben-Scafidi.pdf
14 John Hattie, "What Doesn't Work in Education: The Politics Of Distraction," *Pearson Education*

Money is a necessity in education, but how that money is spent is even more important.

The problem is systemic.

The more political the system becomes, the more rules and regulations will be put in place; the more rules put into place, the more administrators needed to oversee, and enforce, more rules. As more administrators are hired then more money is needed; more administrators result in more people with ideas for new rules, resulting in the need for even more administrators.

The more political the system gets, the greater the administrative bloat. Then with administrative growth, the system gets even more political. It becomes a vicious cycle which feeds on itself as it grows. Slowly, year after year, and decade after decade, the bloat thrives. At the same time, kids and teachers are caught in the political crossfire.

To make a name for themselves, and to prove their self-worth, school administrators, superintendents, education professors, and other experts have an incentive to come up with new ideas to supposedly improve education. Unfortunately, too often they then impose these new fads on the teachers and students regardless of proven success or failure. "If you cannot think of more rules yourself, keep adopting the latest management fad. No matter how stupid it is and how stupid it sounds...."[15]

If you can't think of a new fad, just repackage and rename an old one.

15   Hans-Georg Michna, *In Search of Inefficiency*, How to Secure Jobs By Being Inefficient; http://michna.com/inefficiency.htm

Management control from afar requires the adoption and adherence of rules, standards, and procedures. Throughout the 20th century, standards and procedures were developed and implemented based on production-line concepts. In order for the production line to work, kids were grouped by age, while bureaucrats from afar determined what curriculum and curriculum fads should be delivered to each age group. The teacher was directed to simply input the data, as determined from above, at the appropriate time.

Experts and administrators attempted to design and oversee an education system optimized by production techniques to hopefully maximize efficiency. Instead, however, that system has driven gross inefficiency, as discussed above. Individualized education was minimized, teacher innovation was stifled, and classroom teachers were treated more like production workers than professionals.

Rules matter, money matters, and the structure of the system matters a lot. But there is a sharp contrast between the administrative staffing needs of an excessive top-down system and other, more efficient, structural alternatives. For example: "The New York City public school system has 250 times as many administrators as the New York Catholic school system (6,000 administrators in the public school system versus 24 in the Catholic school system), even though New York public schools have only four times as many students as the Catholic schools….

"…it's no surprise that Catholic schools don't suffer from 'administrative bloat' to the extent public schools do."[16]

---

16   American Enterprise Institute; http://www.aei.org/publication/chart-of-the-day-administrative-bloat-in-us-public-schools/

If kids were truly the priority, the New York public schools would not suffer such administrative bloat.

With the massive growth in public school administration around the country, spending priorities have become significantly misaligned with the educational needs and priorities of both students and teachers. "Overall school funding increased dramatically on a per-student basis, quadrupling in real dollars between 1960 and 2015."[17] And yet at the same time, "Teacher salaries have declined relative to those earned by other four-year college-degree holders and are currently low relative to comparable workers in other occupations."[18]

The system, as structured today, simply targets the wrong priorities. The current system is designed to fund the education system rather than to fund education within the system. In the 22 years between 1992 and 2014, national spending for teachers, adjusted for inflation, only increased by 28%. However, spending for non-teacher staff increased by 45% in real inflation-adjusted dollars.[19] Resources are not being allocated wisely.

The system is designed to fund the education system rather than to fund education within the system.

---

17   The Achievement Gap Fails to Close, Eric Hanushek and Paul Peterson, Summer 2019; http://hanushek.stanford.edu/sites/default/files/publications/Hanushek%20et%20al.%202019%20EdNext%2019%283%29.pdf
18   ibid
19   Back to the Staffing Surge, Benjamin Scafidi, Ph.D., May 2017; https://www.edchoice.org/wp-content/uploads/2017/06/Back-to-the-Staffing-Surge-by-Ben-Scafidi.pdf

Resource allocation will determine the success or failure of any endeavor. Resources dedicated to productive efforts will always yield greater success than resources allocated unwisely.

The restructuring of public education that occurred in the early 20th century set the stage for today's system, which disproportionately allocates resources towards non-productive oversight activities. Without question, decisions regarding resource allocations within today's education system are driven by politics. Such political decisions are animated not only by political forces but also by the structures of the system itself, and the financing mechanisms used to fund the system.

Today, education finance, throughout the nation, is ill-aligned with student needs, and is ill-aligned to maximize professional staffing in the classroom. Teachers, students, taxpayers, and society in general would be much better served if resources were being allocated as effectively as possible toward achieving educational excellence. The current structure, with excessive top-down control, discourages rather than encourages such efficiency.

Today, teachers are not in control of education. Parents, unless they serve on the school board, are not in control. Politicians, bureaucrats, and administrators determine what they think is best for students around the country. Those decisions are acceptable to many, yet many students and teachers are allowed to fall through the cracks. We must explore ideas which will set teachers free and once again allow teachers and parents greater control over the education of their students/children. We will explore such ideas in future chapters.

CHAPTER 3

A System at Risk

> We're living in the 21st century while insisting on an education architecture built for the 1800s.... It's time to construct an entirely new system.
>
> —Texas Governor Greg Abbott

Public education, as we know it in America, is at risk. Although teachers across the country are working hard, the system has not produced results commensurate with those efforts, and the system fails to adequately support and reward teachers.[20] Although many significant education reform efforts have been implemented over the past half-century (a topic to be discussed later) almost all of those reform efforts have been top-down approaches demanding changes from upon-high with little input from classroom teachers.

From our founding, the purpose of public education was the general diffusion of knowledge. Many of our founding fathers, at both the state and federal levels, associated ignorance with

---

20 "Teacher salaries have declined relative to those earned by other four-year college-degree holders and are currently low relative to comparable workers in other occupations." *The Achievement Gap Fails to Close*, Eric Hanushek and Paul Peterson, Summer 2019; http://hanushek.stanford.edu/sites/default/files/publications/Hanushek%20et%20al.%202019%20EdNext%2019%283%29.pdf

tyranny; therefore, education—a general diffusion of knowledge—was seen as the critical pathway to sustained freedom. They developed founding documents with this in mind.[21] Over the past century, that focus has changed as the system itself has become the central emphasis.

Let us review some of the issues that might place the public education system, as we know it today, at risk:

- An unacceptable achievement gap between white and minority students;
- Less than stellar overall student achievement levels when compared to international achievement levels;
- Public concern and discontent with perceived inefficiencies;
- Changing political dynamics, and growing politicization of our schools;
- High property taxes;
- Growth in private and home school enrollment, confirming public discontent;
- Demographic changes such as an aging population less willing to fund what they perceive as inefficiencies in the system.

Some of these concerns have greater merit than others. Let us examine each of these issues.

---

21 Encyclopedia.com; https://www.encyclopedia.com/history/encyclopedias-almanacs-transcripts-and-maps/public-education

Achievement Gap Between White and Minority Students

Black students in many states, especially in inner-city schools, are not performing well. As seen in the chart below, in some states, a majority of black students are failing to meet standards. In fact, 83% of California's African-American students failed to meet standards in 2017.[22] Disproportionate failure to meet standards has been a continuing problem for both the black and Hispanic communities around the nation for decades.

Over the past four or five decades there have been significant attempts to equalize education funding to assure enhanced opportunities for poor students. However, at the same time, the lack of productivity and efficiency in our schools has disproportionately harmed the poor.[23]

The poorest students in America perform three or four years behind their wealthiest counterparts. Although for some subgroups progress has been made, the poverty achievement gap has actually remained unchanged for the past half-century.[24]

The poorest students in America perform three or four years behind.

---

22 "Black Minds Matter," *Medium, Tipping Point*, April 18, 2018; https://medium.com/tipping-point/black-minds-matter-and-how-data-helps-close-the-achievement-gap-132bb431153f
23 *The Declining Productivity of Education,* The Brookings Institution, December 2016; https://www.brookings.edu/blog/social-mobility-memos/2016/12/23/the-declining-productivity-of-education/
24 Achievement Gaps, *Education Week*, August 14, 2019; https://www.edweek.org/ew/articles/2019/04/10/achievement-gaps-1.html

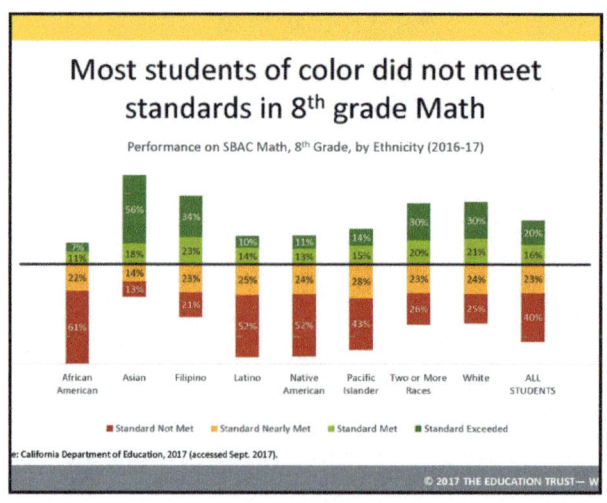

Chart included courtesy of Education Trust. Chart also found at: "Black Minds Matter," *Medium, Tipping Point*, April 18, 2018; https://medium.com/tipping-point/black-minds-matter-and-how-data-helps-close-the-achievement-gap-132bb431153f

As one expert explained: "All sorts of ideas—and money—have been thrown at the problem: Head Start, services for students with disabilities, more equal funding for school districts, an overall quadrupling in per-student spending. But none of that has worked." She then goes on to explain that the black-white gap has "not changed over the past two decades." She concludes that "It's time to stop attacking the problem with reform strategies that haven't worked."[25]

Unquestionably, a new approach is needed to close the achievement gap. One suggestion is to set individual teachers free to tackle the problem on an individual student-needs basis

---

25   The Achievement Gap Hasn't Budged in 50 Years. Now What? Natalie Wexler, Forbes Mar 17, 2019; https://www.forbes.com/sites/nataliewexler/2019/03/17/the-achievement-gap-hasnt-budged-in-50-years-now-what/#1cc4839b4d90

instead of "forcing a stringent, systemic approach" on both the teacher and student.

As another observer noted: "We can build on children's strengths by supporting them and challenging them to excel. The good news is that closing the opportunity gap doesn't require a magical quick fix; the bad news is that to do it we need to stop grasping at those magical quick fixes."[26]

Although much effort has been made to close the achievement gap, it remains at a level completely intolerable and with far too little measurable progress. Many reforms have targeted this problem with little overall success. Individual teachers who are dedicated, and allowed to practice their trade, are the most important component to student achievement,[27] and therefore have made greater progress in closing the achievement gap for minority students than have most top-down mandates.

International Status

The other achievement gap is the gap between test scores for American students when compared to our international counterparts in developed nations. America's schools do not rate as highly as we would like when compared to international student test scores. According to data collected by the Organization for Economic Cooperation and Development (OECD) **America places 25th out of 78 industrialized nations** in scholastic

---

26 What Is the Achievement Gap and What Can Educators Do About It? Ashley Abramson, 2/21/18; https://www.rasmussen.edu/degrees/education/blog/what-is-the-achievement-gap/
27 Effective teachers are the most important factor contributing to student achievement, *Educational Research Newsletter*; https://www.ernweb.com/educational-research-articles/effective-teachers-are-the-most-important-factor-contributing-to-student-achievement/

performance of 15-year-old students on math, science, and reading.

America places 37th out of 78 industrialized nations on math.
– International PISA scores 2019

Even more concerning, the **United States places 37th on math scores**—the core subject for engineering and technical occupations, which play a key role in economic development. The nations which outperform America on math scores include: China, Singapore, Macao, Hong Kong, Taiwan, Japan, South Korea, Estonia, Netherlands, Poland, Switzerland, Canada, Denmark, Slovenia, Belgium, Finland, Sweden, United Kingdom, Norway, Germany, Ireland, Austria, Czechia, Latvia, France, Iceland, New Zealand, Portugal, Australia, Russia, Italy, Slovakia, Luxembourg, Hungary, Lithuania, and Spain (see math chart below).

"The U.S. is actually the exception, not the norm, in that we have plodded along at the same level for decades as other countries pass us by."[28] Leading the world in overall student results (for math, science, and reading) are several Asian countries. China, Singapore, Macao, and Hong Kong occupy the top four positions.

The only European nation to make the top 5, in overall results, was Estonia. (More on Estonia later.) The other nations that also outperform America in math, reading, and science are: Japan, South Korea, Canada, Finland, Poland, Ireland,

---

28   Jonah Edelman, CEO Stand For Children; http://stand.org/national/blog/2013/08/12/smartest-kids-world-and-how-they-got-way

Slovenia, United Kingdom, New Zealand, Netherlands, Sweden, Denmark, Germany, Belgium, Australia, Switzerland, Norway, Czechia.[29] See the complete results in the charts below.

The Program for International Student Assessment (PISA) is a worldwide study by OECD in 77 nations of 15-year-old students' scholastic performance on mathematics, science, and reading.

International PISA Math Scores:

1.	China (Beijing, Shanghai, Jiangsu, Zhejiang)	591
2.	Singapore	569
3.	Macao	558
4.	Hong Kong, China	551
5.	Taiwan	531
6.	Japan	527
7.	South Korea	526
8.	Estonia	523
9.	Netherlands	519
10.	Poland	516
11.	Switzerland	515
12.	Canada	512
13.	Denmark	509
	Slovenia	509
15.	Belgium	508
16.	Finland	507
17.	Sweden	502
	United Kingdom	502
19.	Norway	501
20.	Germany	500

---

29 PISA Worldwide Rankings; http://factsmaps.com/pisa-worldwide-ranking-average-score-of-math-science-reading/

	Ireland	500
22.	Austria	499
	Czechia	499
24.	Latvia	496
25.	France	495
	Iceland	495
27.	New Zealand	494
28.	Portugal	492
29.	Australia	491
30.	Russia	488
31.	Italy	487
32.	Slovakia	486
33.	Luxembourg	483
34.	Hungary	481
	Lithuania	481
	Spain	481
37.	**United States**	**478**
38.	Malta	472
	Belarus	472
40.	Croatia	464
41.	Israel	463
42.	Turkey	454
43.	Ukraine	453
44.	Cyprus	451
	Greece	451
46.	Serbia	448
47.	Malaysia	440
48.	Albania	437
49.	Bulgaria	436
50.	United Arab Emirates	435
51.	Brunei	430
	Romania	430
	Montenegro	430
54.	Kazakhstan	423

55.	Moldova	421
56.	Azerbaijan	420
57.	Thailand	419
58.	Uruguay	418
59.	Chile	417
60.	Qatar	414
61.	Mexico	409
62.	Bosnia and Herzegovina	406
63.	Costa Rica	402
64.	Jordan	400
	Peru	400
66.	Georgia	398
67.	North Macedonia	394
68.	Lebanon	393
69.	Colombia	391
70.	Brazil	384
71.	Argentina	379
	Indonesia	379
73.	Saudi Arabia	373
74.	Morocco	368
75.	Kosovo	366
76.	Panama	353
	Philippines	353
78	Dominican Republic	325

Chart From: PISA Worldwide Rankings; http://factsmaps.com/pisa-worldwide-ranking-average-score-of-math-science-reading/

International PISA Science Scores:

1.	China (Beijing, Shanghai, Jiangsu, Zhejiang)	590
2.	Singapore	551
3.	Macao	544
4.	Estonia	530

5.	Japan	529
6.	Finland	522
7.	South Korea	519
8.	Canada	518
9.	Hong Kong, China	517
10.	Taiwan	516
11.	Poland	511
12.	New Zealand	508
13.	Slovenia	507
14.	United Kingdom	505
15.	Australia	503
	Germany	503
	Netherlands	503
18.	**United States**	**502**
19.	Belgium	499
	Sweden	499
21.	Czechia	497
22.	Ireland	496
23.	Switzerland	495
24.	Denmark	493
	France	493
26.	Portugal	492
27.	Austria	490
	Norway	490
29.	Latvia	487
30.	Spain	483
31.	Lithuania	482
32.	Hungary	481
33.	Russia	478
34.	Luxembourg	477
35.	Iceland	475
36.	Croatia	472
37.	Belarus	471
38.	Ukraine	469

39.	Italy	468
	Turkey	468
41.	Slovakia	464
42.	Israel	462
43.	Malta	457
44.	Greece	452
45.	Chile	444
46.	Serbia	440
47.	Cyprus	439
48.	Malaysia	438
49.	United Arab Emirates	434
50.	Brunei	431
51.	Jordan	429
52.	Moldova	428
53.	Romania	426
54.	Thailand	426
	Uruguay	426
56.	Bulgaria	424
57.	Mexico	419
	Qatar	419
59.	Albania	417
60.	Costa Rica	416
61.	Montenegro	415
62.	Colombia	413
	North Macedonia	413
64.	Argentina	404
	Brazil	404
	Peru	404
67.	Azerbaijan	398
	Bosnia and Herzegovina	398
69.	Kazakhstan	397
70.	Indonesia	396
71.	Saudi Arabia	386
72.	Lebanon	384

73.	Georgia	383
74.	Morocco	377
75.	Kosovo	365
	Panama	365
77.	Philippines	357

Chart From: PISA Worldwide Rankings; http://factsmaps.com/pisa-worldwide-ranking-average-score-of-math-science-reading/

International PISA Reading Scores:

1.	China (Beijing, Shanghai, Jiangsu, Zhejiang)	555
2.	Singapore	549
3.	Macao	525
4.	Hong Kong, China	524
5.	Estonia	523
6.	Canada	520
7.	Finland	520
8.	Ireland	518
9.	South Korea	514
10.	Poland	512
11.	New Zealand	506
	Sweden	506
13.	**United States**	**505**
14.	Japan	504
	United Kingdom	504
16.	Australia	503
	Taiwan	503
18.	Denmark	501
19.	Norway	499
20.	Germany	498
21.	Slovenia	495
22.	Belgium	493
	France	493

24.	Portugal	492
25.	Czechia	490
26.	Netherlands	485
27.	Switzerland	484
	Austria	484
29.	Croatia	479
	Latvia	479
	Russia	479
32.	Hungary	476
	Italy	476
	Lithuania	476
35.	Iceland	474
	Belarus	474
37.	Israel	470
	Luxembourg	470
39.	Turkey	466
	Ukraine	466
41.	Slovakia	458
42.	Greece	457
43.	Chile	452
44.	Malta	448
45.	Serbia	439
46.	United Arab Emirates	432
47.	Romania	428
48.	Uruguay	427
49.	Costa Rica	426
50.	Cyprus	424
	Moldova	424
52.	Montenegro	421
53.	Bulgaria	420
	Mexico	420
55.	Jordan	419
56.	Malaysia	415
57.	Brazil	413

58.	Colombia	412
59.	Brunei	408
60.	Qatar	407
61.	Albania	405
62.	Bosnia and Herzegovina	403
63.	Argentina	402
64.	Peru	401
65.	Saudi Arabia	399
66.	North Macedonia	393
	Thailand	393
68.	Azerbaijan	389
69.	Kazakhstan	387
70.	Georgia	380
71.	Panama	377
72.	Indonesia	371
73.	Morocco	359
74.	Kosovo	353
	Lebanon	353
76.	Dominican Republic	342
77.	Philippines	340

Chart From: PISA Worldwide Rankings; http://factsmaps.com/pisa-worldwide-ranking-average-score-of-math-science-reading/

Average Combined Score of International PISA For Math, Science and Reading:

1.	China (Beijing, Shanghai, Jiangsu, Zhejiang)	578.7
2.	Singapore	556.3
3.	Macao	542.3
4.	Hong Kong, China	530.7
5.	Estonia	525.3
6.	Japan	520.0
7.	South Korea	519.7

8.	Canada	516.7
	Taiwan	516.7
10.	Finland	516.3
11.	Poland	513.0
12.	Ireland	504.7
13.	Slovenia	503.7
	United Kingdom	503.7
15.	New Zealand	502.7
16.	Netherlands	502.3
	Sweden	502.3
18.	Denmark	501.0
19.	Germany	500.3
20.	Belgium	500.0
21.	Australia	499.0
22.	Switzerland	498.0
23.	Norway	496.7
24.	Czechia	495.3
25.	**United States**	**495.0**
26.	France	493.7
27.	Portugal	492.0
28.	Austria	491.0
29.	Latvia	487.3
30.	Russia	481.7
31.	Iceland	481.3
32.	Lithuania	479.7
33.	Hungary	479.3
34.	Italy	477.0
35.	Luxembourg	476.7
36.	Belarus	472.3
37.	Croatia	471.7
38.	Slovakia	469.3
39.	Israel	465.0
40.	Turkey	462.7
	Ukraine	462.7

42.	Malta	459.0
43.	Greece	453.3
44.	Serbia	442.3
45.	Cyprus	438.0
46.	Chile	437.7
47.	United Arab Emirates	433.7
48.	Malaysia	431.0
49.	Romania	428.0
50.	Bulgaria	426.7
51.	Moldova	424.3
52.	Uruguay	423.7
53.	Brunei	423.0
54.	Montenegro	422.0
55.	Albania	419.7
56.	Jordan	416.0
	Mexico	416.0
58.	Costa Rica	414.7
59.	Qatar	413.3
60.	Thailand	412.7
61.	Colombia	405.3
62.	Kazakhstan	402.3
	Azerbaijan	402.3
64.	Bosnia and Herzegovina	402.3
65.	Peru	401.7
66.	Brazil	400.3
67.	North Macedonia	400.0
68.	Argentina	395.0
69.	Georgia	387.0
70.	Saudi Arabia	386.0
71.	Indonesia	382.0
72.	Lebanon	376.7
73.	Morocco	368.0
74.	Panama	365.0
75.	Kosovo	361.3

76.	Philippines	350.0
77.	Dominican Republic	334.3

Chart From: PISA Worldwide Rankings; http://factsmaps.com/pisa-worldwide-ranking-average-score-of-math-science-reading/

According to a study by The Brookings Institute, "For the nation's 17-year-olds, there have been no gains in literacy since the National Assessment of Educational Progress began in 1971. Performance is somewhat better on math, but there has still been no progress since 1990. The long-term stagnation cannot be attributed to racial or ethnic differences in the U.S. population. Literacy scores for white students peaked in 1975; in math, scores peaked in the early 1990s.... This weak performance is even more disturbing given that the U.S. spends more on education, on a per student basis, than almost any other country."[30]

There have been no gains in literacy since the National Assessment of Educational Progress began in 1971.

Bottom line: Although we spend a lot, we do not pay teachers well, do not score well by international comparisons, and "our high school graduation rate is now below that of about 20 other nations."[31]

---

30 *The Declining Productivity of Education*, The Brookings Institution, December 2016; https://www.brookings.edu/blog/social-mobility-memos/2016/12/23/the-declining-productivity-of-education/
31 Amanda Ripley, author of *The Smartest Kids in the World and How They Got that Way*, in NPR interview; https://www.npr.org/templates/story/story.php?storyId=217641034

Sidebar: Estonia

The Republic of Estonia is a country on the eastern coast of the Baltic Sea in Northern Europe. It was formerly a part of the Soviet Union (USSR), but is now rated among top countries in terms of economic freedom,[32] and in 2017 the average monthly salary in Estonia was 1,221 Euros (about $1,111 in U.S. dollars)[33]. Nevertheless, Estonia has the lowest percentage of low-performing students in the world[34], and its students consistently perform in the top tier as measured by international test scores.

So why does this small, largely unknown country excel in student performance as compared to all other European societies? One key component appears to be autonomy, at the national, local, and classroom levels. Teachers, parents, and administrators are guaranteed a great deal of latitude regarding the education of school age children.

Estonia has small average class sizes; however, this is in part due to many very small schools with students of varying ages in the same classroom. Therefore, it is difficult to attribute the country's success to class size, especially since Japan outscores most nations with an average class size of 40 students.

---

32 Foundation for Economic Education, March 23, 2018; https://fee.org/articles/how-estonia-yes-estonia-became-one-of-the-wealthiest-countries-in-eastern-europe/

33 Workinestonia.com, September 2018; https://www.workinestonia.com/salary-levels-and-everydays-costs-in-estonia/

34 Thomas Hatch, 10 Surprises in the High-Performing Estonian Education System, *International Education News*, August 2, 2017; https://internationalednews.com/2017/08/02/10-surprises-in-the-high-performing-estonian-education-system/

Estonia guarantees early childhood education and after school programs for all children. Ninety percent of three to seven-year-olds participate in the early childhood education program[35]. Estonia provides funding for at least one hobby school activity each week. These activities consist of things like the arts, sports, technology, culture, music, etc. As with all education, pre-school, as well as hobby school programs, are provided by both public and private providers in Estonia.

High-stakes testing in Estonia is limited primarily to high school exit exams. The exit exam data is made public and commonly published in local newspapers. Most other testing is done on a sample basis, with results being confidential. School accountability in Estonia, as compared to school accountability in America, is much more limited, much more localized, more targeted to graduation requirements, and more effective overall.

In Estonia, "...schools, school leaders, and teachers have a considerable amount of autonomy. Schools have to provide a minimum number of course hours in set subjects, but they also have some latitude in emphasizing a particular focus like the arts, technology, or the natural sciences." However, students have a lot of latitude and can focus more on math, science, or the arts.

Although 95% of students attend public schools, Estonia offers much in the form of school choice. Students can attend schools outside their geographic districts, both public and private. "In most private schools, tuition is largely subsidized by the state, but schools can also charge additional fees that can make them out of reach for some students. Some of the private schools are religious schools or international schools, but in recent years, a variety of other groups have started [their] own private schools. I spoke with the founders of two different private schools who both described how parents got together to create schools when they were unhappy with their local options."[36]

The key to Estonia's success is most likely the freedom and autonomy granted to teachers and administrators. Since they have the flexibility to adjust to student needs, the public schools, and public school teachers, have great ability to meet the actual needs of students. Without this autonomy, and the ability of parents to move their children elsewhere, it is doubtful Estonia would rank so high by international standards, nor would the public schools be able to maintain the high 95% participation enrollment figures.

35 ibid
36 ibid

In Estonia parents can create new schools when they are unhappy with their local options.

Public Concern: A Nation at Risk?

As noted earlier, there is significant public concern regarding the achievement gap and also significant concern that America's status in international student performance overall is disappointing. If you talk with young mothers today, a major concern is how they can ensure that their children receive an appropriate education. Some do so by enrolling their children in private schools; others move to neighborhoods with superior public schools. Real estate values in areas with better schools are significantly higher than those in areas with poor performing schools. Education is very important to the general public.

I have never let my schooling interfere with my education.
– Mark Twain

However, only one in six Texas high school graduates are college ready as determined by SAT and ACT test scores. Sadly, of the Texas high school graduates who go on to college, 40% require remediation[37]. Most states face similar circumstances, as noted below. Taxpayers are paying twice; they are funding high schools and then required to fund the remediation of many students once they enroll in college.

---

37 *Texas Commission on Public School Finance Report*, 2018

Taxpayers are paying twice.

Some indication of these public concerns are demonstrated in the following quotes:

> "The failure to hold elected officials responsible for school quality trickles down to the entire system. Voters don't make politicians pay, and politicians do not make school systems pay. Few schools or educators face consequences for low performance."[38]

> "Meanwhile, about 1 in 5 students never graduates from high school; 2 out of 3 who do graduate are not ready for college; among those who go to college, 1 in 4 needs to retake high school classes at their own expense; and 40 percent of college students do not finish within six years, costing parents, students and taxpayers billions.

> "Education is arguably the most important investment society makes. It's the surest path to the American Dream for people of every race and background. Every problem we face, from joblessness and crime to racism and even obesity, can be better addressed through education. Successful graduates contribute to society. Unsuccessful students carry costs."[39]

Such public concerns and frustrations are not new. In 1957 the Russians beat America by putting the first man into space with their Sputnik satellite. That caused national concern and was the impetus for new federally mandated education reform efforts. Congress passed, and President Eisenhower signed,

---

38 Is Politics the Problem in Education or the Solution? Peter Cunningham, *Education Post*, April 13, 2017; https://education-post.org/is-politics-the-problem-in-education-or-the-solution/
39 ibid

the *National Defense Education Act* in 1958 as one of many reform efforts intended to improve education in America. Also, reformers around the country enacted significant curriculum reforms designed to improve math and science education in attempts to counter the perceived Russian threat.

In 1965 President Johnson, himself a former teacher, signed into law the *Elementary and Secondary Education Act* that allocated significant federal money for the public education system. Then in 1983, during the Reagan administration, the nation was declared at risk due to the failures of the education system. In 1983 the *A Nation at Risk* report issued by the National Commission on Excellence in Education concluded: "If an unfriendly foreign power had attempted to impose on America the mediocre educational performance that exists today, we might well have viewed it as an act of war."[40]

"If an unfriendly foreign power had attempted to impose on America the mediocre educational performance that exists today, we might well have viewed it as an act of war."

– *A Nation at Risk*, U.S. Department of Education 1983

In 2001 the federal government took perhaps its biggest step to insert itself into the public education system of America. With a great deal of help from Senator Ted Kennedy, President George W. Bush signed into law the *No Child Left Behind Act*. "We're gonna spend more money, more resources," Bush said at the time, "but they'll be directed at methods that work. Not feel-good methods. Not sound-good methods. But methods

---

40   U.S. Department of Education, A Nation At Risk, April 1983; https://www2.ed.gov/pubs/NatAtRisk/risk.html

that actually work."[41] The goal was to have every single student in America performing at grade level in reading and math by 2014. That goal was obviously not achieved, even though the federal government appropriated billions of dollars to achieve the objective.

These examples are from the federal level, and they represent the overall concern and focus on education reform at this level. Likewise, every state has attempted to improve education at the state and local levels over the last half-century. As noted earlier, per-pupil spending has increased 400% over the past 60 years in real dollars, while teacher's salaries have declined relative to other professionals.

In 2001 the stated federal goal was for all kids to read at grade level by 2014, a goal never reached.

The common problem with all these reform efforts is that they are all based on a top-down leadership approach. Mandates from above will never solve the perceived education crisis in America. Hard-working teachers, not bureaucrats and politicians, are the only ones who can attain the desired results. They can only do so when they are set free to do their jobs, and only when they are rewarded accordingly.

The nation is still at risk today.

---

41   NPR, No Child Left Behind: What Worked, What Didn't, October 27, 2015; https://www.npr.org/sections/ed/2015/10/27/443110755/no-child-left-behind-what-worked-what-didnt

Public Perception of Systemic Inefficiencies

Another risk to the public education system is the perception that today's top-down public education system is rife with inefficiencies. Unfortunately, politicians sometimes screw things up. In legitimate attempts to solve problems, politicians pass laws and implement rules that inevitably result in unintended consequences. When common sense decisions become secondary to rules, then such decisions will inevitably lead to rule driven inefficiencies and, therefore, poor results.

Politicians sometimes screw things up.

When bad consequences occur due to flawed rules, instead of eliminating the inferior rules, politicians and bureaucrats just write new rules in attempts to solve rule-based problems; new rules then lead to still other unintended consequences. This process becomes like a revolving door: As new problems are discovered, they adopt additional rules to deal with the new issue. Thus, the rulebook grows and common sense is repressed even more. Of course, as the rulebook grows, so must the bureaucracy necessary to implement and oversee the rules. The end result is less control by the teacher, less common sense, greater control from above, and more administrative growth. Good people trying to do good often do even more harm.

The result: Less control by teachers; less common sense; more control from above; and more administrative growth.

Administrative bloat and bureaucratic rules contribute to a common perception that the system is inherently inefficient. That perception is justified due to growth in school administration as outlined above, and the failure to allocate sufficient funds directly to the classroom effort. In primary and secondary public education "there has been a decline in bureaucratic efficiency"[42] over many decades.

Efficiency is an important component to success in any endeavor. Many states, including Arkansas, Delaware, Illinois, Kentucky, Maryland, New Jersey, Ohio, Pennsylvania, Texas, and West Virginia, require an "efficient" system of public education in their state constitutions.[43] However, none seem to actually require the efficiencies their respective founders intended.

The dynamics within the system actually discourage, rather than encourage, efficiency. Politicians inherently need to legislate, and bureaucrats inherently need to administer. Therefore, the administrative portion of the school system continues to grow at rates greater than both student and teacher growth rates, as demonstrated earlier.

Excessive administrative growth is inherently inefficient. The one thing every bureaucracy has in common is the desire to protect itself and to grow itself. As former Texas Education Commissioner Raymond Bynum once said: "Far too many people in public education view the education system as a jobs program rather than an education program."

In addition to administrative bloat, many others profit from the public education system today. Billions of dollars are at

---

42 *The Declining Productivity of Education*, The Brookings Institution, December 2016; https://www.brookings.edu/blog/social-mobility-memos/2016/12/23/the-declining-productivity-of-education/
43 Hartman, Constitutional Responsibility To Provide A System Of Free Public Schools; https://surface.syr.edu/cgi/viewcontent.cgi?article=1348&context=jilc

stake. We spend $4 billion per school day in America on primary and secondary education.[44]

We spend $4 billion per day on public education.

Four billion dollars per day is a huge pot of gold and many people and organizations want their share of that pot of taxpayer money. Since most decisions are driven by politics, thousands of lobbyists around the country are retained by school systems, school districts, or other organizations that survive on school system funding.

Thousands of people work for associations affiliated with education, and thousands work in the various bureaucracies that oversee or serve the public education bureaucracy. Schools pay consultants to massage data and finance formulas in manners that will maximize funding based on very complex funding models.

Bottom line: **Virtually all these people profit from the system significantly more than do the teachers** who actually deliver the services. Complex rules and regulations assure that these non-productive jobs will continue to be necessary.

Non-productive people profit more from the system than do the teachers who actually produce the results.

Unfortunately, in addition to rules and regulations adopted by state and local governments, the federal government has become more involved in educational matters over recent

---

[44] Nationally we spent $706 billion in 2016; typical school year is 180 days.

decades, as noted above. In order to collect more federal dollars, states and districts must abide by federal rules. One big advantage private schools and private school teachers have is the fact that federal laws do not interfere with their educational decisions. Excessive rules and regulations put the public education system at a competitive disadvantage and increases overall inefficiency within the system.

Although the federal government only provides a small portion of overall school funding—about 8% of total K-12 funding[45]—they drive a significantly larger portion of expenditures and administrative costs. School systems outside such federal mandates offer significant savings that could be reallocated to the classroom in a properly structured system.

Politics in Schools

Without question, politics dominate American education. The perception that education is being used to promote specific political agendas also presents a risk to public education. Since progressives who dominate the schools of education in America train most teachers[46], and most organizations that represent teachers at the local, state, and national level consistently promote liberal agendas, many Americans have expressed concern that the education establishment has unnecessarily politicized education.

In addition, many teachers are unhappy with the perceived political bias of their profession, and the organizations that

---

45 *Governing*, June 4, 2019, "States That Spend Most (and least) on Education;" https://www.governing.com/topics/education/gov-state-education-spending-revenue-data.html

46 David F. Labaree, "Progressivism, Schools and Schools of Education: An American Romance," *Paedagogica Historica, Vol. 41, Nos. 1&2, pp. 275-288*

represent them. Most teachers, however, keep their frustrations to themselves.

The question is: Is public education changing society or is society changing education? A 2019 *Wall Street Journal*/NBC poll found that millennials do not value patriotism, religion, or family as did their predecessors.

The poll found that over the past 21 years the importance of religion has declined by 12%, the importance of patriotism declined by 9%, and the importance of having children declined by 16%. More concerning are results for young people 18-38: Only 42% think patriotism is very important, as compared to 80% for those over 55 years of age. Further, although the older group felt that religion was very important by a two to one margin, only one in three of the 18-38-year-olds feel this way.[47]

Despite the history of socialism's economic and political failures throughout world history, including the early days in America, 2019 polling indicates that a majority of 18-24-year-olds prefer

---

47 "Americans Have Shifted Dramatically on What Values Matter Most," *Wall Street Journal*, August 25, 2019; https://www.wsj.com/articles/americans-have-shifted-dramatically-on-what-values-matter-most-11566738001

socialism to capitalism.[48] This finding is very alarming to many Americans and causes them to question what is being taught in our colleges and in our public schools.

Frustration with our schools, and the potential propagandizing of public education, has been expressed by many, including George Will, who editorialized in the *Washington Post*, "The real vocation of some people entrusted with delivering primary and secondary education is to validate this proposition: The three R's — formerly reading, 'riting and 'rithmetic — now are racism, reproduction and recycling... [many school bureaucrats] evidently considers 'instruction' synonymous with 'propaganda,' which in the patois of progressivism is called 'consciousness-raising' .... No corner of the country is immune to propaganda pretending to be pedagogy."[49]

---

48   Gen Z prefers "socialism" to "capitalism", Jan 27, 2019, *Axios*; https://www.axios.com/socialism-capitalism-poll-generation-z-preference-1ffb8800-0ce5-4368-8a6f-de3b82662347.html
49   George Will, Schools push a curriculum of propaganda, *Washington Post*, April 3, 2013; https://www.washingtonpost.com/opinions/george-f-will-schools-push-a-curriculum-of-propaganda/2013/04/03/6d25550e-9bc1-11e2-a941-a19bce7af755_story.html

Considering the reality that public education is totally driven by politics, it is politically unhealthy for the public education system in-block to be viewed as taking sides. Doing so puts the entire system at future risk.

High Property Taxes

Property taxes are very unpopular with the general public. Resistance to ever growing property taxes creates a significant future risk to funding for public education.

> **My husband and I finally paid off our mortgage after 30 years, now our tax payments are more than our original mortgage payments. Now, we just rent our home from the government.**

It is not uncommon for someone to finally pay off their home loan after 20 or 30 years of making payments, and then find that their tax payment exceeds their original mortgage payment. In that sense, no one actually ever owns their home; instead they just rent their homes from the government. However, property taxes are a critical component in school funding. The typical state in America relies on local property taxes for about 45% of education funding, another 45% of funding comes from state taxes, and about 10% comes from federal funds.[50]

"Property taxation and school funding are closely linked in the United States, with nearly half of all property tax revenue used for public elementary and secondary education.... States

---

50   Why America's Schools Have A Money Problem. April 18, 2016, NPR; https://www.npr.org/2016/04/18/474256366/why-americas-schools-have-a-money-problem

experiencing taxpayer revolts among homeowners are tempted to reduce reliance on the property tax to fund schools."[51]

Although no tax is popular, the property tax is among the most unpopular tax in existence today. It is more unpopular than federal income taxes, payroll taxes, state income taxes, and state sales taxes.[52] Unfortunately, education is highly dependent on a very unpopular tax for its continuing operations and facilities funding.

Abandonment

Another risk to public education, as we know it today, is the growing number of parents who are losing confidence in public education as an institution and are, therefore, abandoning public education in favor of private and home schooling. Although the number is still relatively low, it is growing. That growth has primarily been reflected by the growth in home schooling. According to one report, "While the overall *school*-age population in the United States grew by about 2.0 percent from spring 2012 to spring 2016, data from 16 states from all four major regions of the nation showed that *homeschooling* grew by an average of about 25 percent in those states."[53]

---

51 The Property Tax-School Funding Dilemma, December 2007, Lincoln Institute of Land Policy; https://www.lincolninst.edu/publications/policy-focus-reports/property-tax-school-funding-dilemma
52 Source: Gallup, April 2005, Justin Fox, Why Economist Love Property Taxes and You Don't, November 28, 2017, Bloomberg Opinion; https://www.bloomberg.com/opinion/articles/2017-11-28/why-economists-love-property-taxes-and-you-don-t
53 Homeschooling Growing: Multiple Data Points Show Increase 2012 to 2016 and Later, April 20, 2018, National Home Education Research Institute; https://www.nheri.org/homeschool-population-size-growing/

According to the National Center for Educational Statistics, home schooling doubled in the first 12 years of the 21st century, growing from 850,000 to 1,800,000 students.[54] Although often seen as a conservative Christian movement, homeschooling was actually first promoted by the countercultural left in the 1970s. Then religious conservatives advanced the movement significantly during the latter part of the 20th century. However, much of "the recent growth in the homeschooling population has occurred among urban, secular families who are disillusioned by increasingly restrictive, test-driven mass schooling and seek a more innovative, progressive, child-centered approach to learning."[55]

As indicated earlier, significant problems exist with our inner-city public schools. Therefore, parental dissatisfaction with those public schools is no surprise. A majority of urban parents are unsatisfied with the quality of education their children receive in public schools, as indicated by the following quote: "Urban parents are less likely to rate local public schools as high quality. Sixty percent of suburban parents say the quality of education in local public high schools is good or excellent compared with only 42 percent of urban parents."[56]

So, many Christian conservatives have chosen to explore homeschooling opportunities due to cultural issues, and a growing number of secular urban parents are exploring homeschooling opportunities due to quality issues. Homeschooling has also

---

54   Kerry McDonald, The Bipartisan Growth of Homeschooling, *Motherly*; https://www.mother.ly/parenting/the-bipartisan-growth-of-homeschooling
55   ibid
56   Parents' Attitudes on the Quality of Education in the United States, *The Associated Press*–NORC Center for Public Affairs Research; http://www.apnorc.org/PDFs/Parent%20Attitudes/AP_NORC_Parents%20Attitudes%20on%20the%20Quality%20of%20Education%20in%20the%20US_FINAL_2.pdf

become more popular because it offers unlimited opportunities for individualized learning and innovation in teaching.

A doubling of homeschooling over 12 years is significant; however, quantifying homeschooling is difficult. One idea that is growing in popularity around the country is the hybrid homeschool model. With the hybrid model, the student will stay at home some days and go to a hybrid school campus on other days of the week—a mixed agenda. It could also mean attendance at school for certain limited hours of a day or week. The scheduling possibilities are unlimited, and some suggest it may be the "wave of the future" in education.

As Mike McShane writes in *Forbes*, "Hybrid homeschools are particularly interesting for two reasons. First, they blur the lines around what we consider a 'school.' With the proliferation of new technologies and resources, it is much easier for families to get high-quality materials and instruction for their children in a wide range of subjects. It is also easier for families to network with each other and find opportunities to collaborate."[57]

Bottom line: "Nearly 2 million kids today are home-schooled by parents who nevertheless still pay taxes for schools they don't use."[58] You may view this as good or bad, but irrespective of that, if this growth continues it could present a risk to the public education system as we know it today.

---

57 Mike McShane, Is Hybrid Homeschooling The Wave Of The Future, *Forbes*, May 21, 2018; https://www.forbes.com/sites/mikemcshane/2018/05/21/is-hybrid-homeschooling-the-wave-of-the-future/#2bc283936bf7
58 Is Politics the Problem in Education or the Solution? Peter Cunningham, *Education Post*, April 13, 2017; https://education-post.org/is-politics-the-problem-in-education-or-the-solution/

Demographic Change

Changing demographics present a potential risk to the public education system in the future. America has an aging population, a population with fewer taxpayers with school age children.[59] Additionally, young people are not having as many children as in the past. An aging population without children in school may be less inclined to support ever-growing school taxes, and an ever-growing school bureaucracy.

Hispanics are the fastest growing population in America. Most are Catholic and many would prefer to send their children to Catholic schools. These demographic shifts could also impact political and tax decisions in the future.

We have explored eight potential risks to public education as it exists today. The unacceptable and lingering achievement gap; inconsequential international student test scores; public concern over five decades; systemic inefficiencies; politicization of our schools; unpopular property taxes; abandonment; and demographic change. When taken as a whole, these issues have the potential, over time, to change the political dynamics that will determine the future of education.

Americans must explore alternatives to the manner by which we structure, fund, and deliver public education. We must find ways to allow and encourage greater innovation. We must find ways to reward teachers fairly. We must find ways to achieve greater efficiency in meeting the needs of students across this great nation.

---

59 6 demographic trends shaping the U.S. and the world in 2019, April 11, 2019, *Pew Research*; https://www.pewresearch.org/fact-tank/2019/04/11/6-demographic-trends-shaping-the-u-s-and-the-world-in-2019/

CHAPTER 4

Merit Pay—A Fool's Errand

> The idea that never works—and never dies. It is the triumph of hope over experience.
> —Diane Ravitch

Business leaders often suggest adding incentives into the public education system in order to increase efficiency. What about performance pay? Diane Ravitch is right when she says that although attempted since the 1920s, merit pay continues to be the "triumph of hope over experience."[60]

Everyone agrees that people should be rewarded for their success; however, **few programs designed to reward teachers for performance have worked well or stood the test of time.** Why? Because attempts to artificially inject market incentives into a top-down system are a fool's errand. Although this author was a big proponent of incentive pay throughout his political career, hindsight provides greater insight.

Teachers do deserve better pay, and great teachers deserve substantially more. The big question is: What is the appropriate solution? Many suggest just increasing teacher pay across the board. Others continue to promote various incentive pay

---

60 Diane Ravitch, *Enterprise Yolo County News*; https://www.davisenterprise.com/local-news/schools-news/education-expert-diane-ravitch-blasts-no-child-left-behind/

plans. Although both are well intended, neither approach alone will likely result in the desired outcomes, nor will either benefit kids in the long term. Why? Because neither of these approaches addresses the underlying structural problem with the way teachers are compensated today.

Everyone should acknowledge one obvious truth: Incentives do matter! However, incentive pay for teachers has consistently resulted in failure, in the long term, when attempted. Although it is not often that this author agrees with teachers' unions, the issue of merit pay for teachers requires serious examination before once again going down that failed path.

Following is a brief review of past attempts to implement teacher incentive pay programs in Texas.

Many education reformers strongly supported the Perot Commission's recommendations passed into law as HB72, and signed by Governor Mark White in the 1980s, especially the incentive pay component known as the Career Ladder. However, the Career Ladder was strongly opposed by the education establishment; therefore, it lasted only a few years before being totally dismantled. In a quarter-century of public service this author personally never observed any particular initiative that was more hated than the Career Ladder—a failed reform effort.

The Career Ladder is a perfect example of this simple fact: There is a huge difference between a good idea and a good law. **Making a good idea work in practical application through a top-down mandate is like trying to thread a needle while blindfolded, and while underwater.**

In 1989 the legislature attempted another incentive program. It promoted and passed a funding program that provided recognition and funds to schools that did a better job of educating kids. Governor Bill Clements and Speaker Gib Lewis supported this program, so it passed even though it was strongly opposed by most of the education establishment, including the chairman of the house education committee. The legislature had successfully injected incentives into the school system. Finally, schools would be recognized and rewarded for doing a good job. Due to continuing opposition from the education establishment, it was watered down in subsequent sessions and eventually became meaningless—another failed reform effort.

In 1995, the Texas Legislature tried again. It inserted a principal's merit pay program into the new re-write of the education code. The program was designed to pay bonuses to principals who produced superior student results on their campuses. Good management should be rewarded, right? Although it was passed into law, due to strong opposition from the education community, Education Commissioner Mike Moses never implemented the program. As a result of continued opposition from the entire education establishment, the program was removed from the education code in the next legislative session without ever being implemented—another failed reform effort.

In 2005 and 2006, a merit-pay reform plan passed out of the Texas House several times, and was finally passed into law in a special session in 2006. Good teachers should be rewarded for their hard work, right? Like all other attempts to inject incentives into the system, the program was hated by the education establishment, and was subsequently altered and watered down to the point it became meaningless—another failed effort to inject incentives into the system.

Prior to passage of that major 2006 reform legislation, reform-minded former school superintendent Forrest Watson visited with the chairman of the House Education Committee. Dr. Watson explained that although merit pay seemed like a common sense solution, it would never work in our politically driven public education system. Of course, believing that they were smarter and that they could design a statewide merit system that would actually work, legislative leaders ignored his counsel. Looking back, Dr. Watson was obviously correct. In ensuing legislative sessions, the program was amended and diluted to totally undermine its intent—another failed reform effort.

Regardless of the value of an education reform proposal, if that idea does not have adequate political support, it will not prevail in the long term. In a politically driven system, political clout will always outweigh virtue and good intent. Governor Mark White was strongly supported by the education community during his 1982 campaign; however, when up for reelection in 1986, those same supporters were upset over the Career Ladder and the other Perot reforms supported by Governor White. The education community took great pride in White's defeat. He had attempted to reform education by forcing change from above. Although these changes made sense to business leaders, they were antithetical to the political preferences of education establishment leaders.

There is a big difference between a good idea and a good law.

We often confuse logic and politics. Just because something, such as performance pay, seems logical does not mean it will work politically. Political power will always trump what would be logical in a non-politically driven system. It is a fool's errand to attempt to inject artificial market dynamics, such as merit pay, into a top-down politically driven system.

Sadly, teachers, students, and taxpayers are all shortchanged by the current politically driven system. The political power of the system will inevitably trump the interest of individual classroom teachers and their students.

It is universally agreed that teachers should be paid better. In considering all costs for facilities, service centers, retirement expenses, and other aspects of the education system, Americans spend about $350,000 per classroom of 25 students.[61] Yet, the average teacher earns only about $60,000. Teachers and their students are grossly undervalued by the system as currently structured. **Education occurs with the teacher in the classroom, yet much of the money is spent elsewhere.** This is neither efficient nor equitable.

No enterprise would be successful if it allocated only 15% to 20% of its revenue to the most important component of its productivity. In education, classroom teachers are where the

---

61   Fast Facts: Expenditures, National Center for Education Statistics; https://nces.ed.gov/fastfacts/display.asp?id=66

action is, yet the percentage allocated to what actually matters, teachers, is embarrassingly low.

The current teacher pay system, based primarily on tenure, is neither fair for teachers nor productive for the system. It is more in line with how assembly-line workers are paid instead of how professionals are normally paid. Pay for performance, simplistically, seems to make a lot of sense; however, as Dr. Watson explained years ago, it will never work as the system is currently structured.

Merit pay is not the solution because it will be abused, undermined, and eventually be undone in a politically driven system. Whereas a market driven system creates its own natural incentives, artificial incentives such a merit pay when injected into a top-down, politically driven system will not work in the long term simply because it is a politically driven system.

Politics will always trump logic.

CHAPTER 5

Teacher Pay

> Teaching is the one profession that creates all other professions.

Teachers will never be rewarded adequately unless we find new ways to unleash and reward their talents. Students and teachers will always be underserved by a system that uses them as political pawns.

Based on real (inflation-adjusted) data, America's public schools have increased spending on a per-student basis by 38% between 1992 and 2017. However, over the same period of time, **real teacher pay has actually decreased by four-tenths of one percent, while spending on non-teaching staff has increased significantly.**[62]

We have immense talent in the education community. We must find ways to set educators free to soar and flourish in a system that truly recognizes and rewards their talents. Instead of giving lip service to teachers as professionals, we must actually allow them to practice their profession in manners best suited for their individual students, and reward them accordingly.

---

62   Dr. Benjamin Scafidi; https://www.edchoice.org/wp-content/uploads/2017/06/Back-to-the-Staffing-Surge-by-Ben-Scafidi.pdf

The biggest reward we could provide to teachers would be to grant them the freedom to practice their profession. The one big difference between the teaching profession and most other professions is the ability of most other professionals to go into private practice.

Teachers are consistently paid less than other professionals. That is because of the way the system is currently structured, which results in school districts having monopsony power over the teaching profession.

Monopsony power is the mirror image of monopoly power. Monopoly power is attained when the seller of goods or services has control over the supply of those goods or services provided. Monopsony power is when the buyer of goods or services has control over which goods or services will be procured. With a monopoly the seller is in control; with a monopsony, the buyer is in control. Since, as structured today, most teachers must sell their services to a school district, school districts have monopsony power over teachers and over teacher salaries.

Dr. Jacob Vigdor, a Harvard trained labor economist, was hired as an expert witness for plaintiff school districts. He provided expert testimony in the Texas school finance case on December 4, 2012 saying that:

> "Introducing greater competition into the market for teachers will raise teacher salaries.... School districts that have power over consumers in the market for education also possess power over teachers in the labor market. They thus represent a classic form of producer with monopsony power. Compared to a competitive labor market—in this context, one where many small education providers compete to hire teachers—monopsonists hire fewer workers and pay them less. They restrict their hiring because in order to hire more workers they would have to pay higher wages—including to the workers already under their employ.

"Intuitively, schools [in a more competitive system] bid up the price of teachers. Thus, while there may be arguments for introducing additional choice for parents, *it must be understood that the classic textbook prediction is that such unleashing of competitive forces would drive up the labor costs of existing schools.*"[63] [Emphasis added]

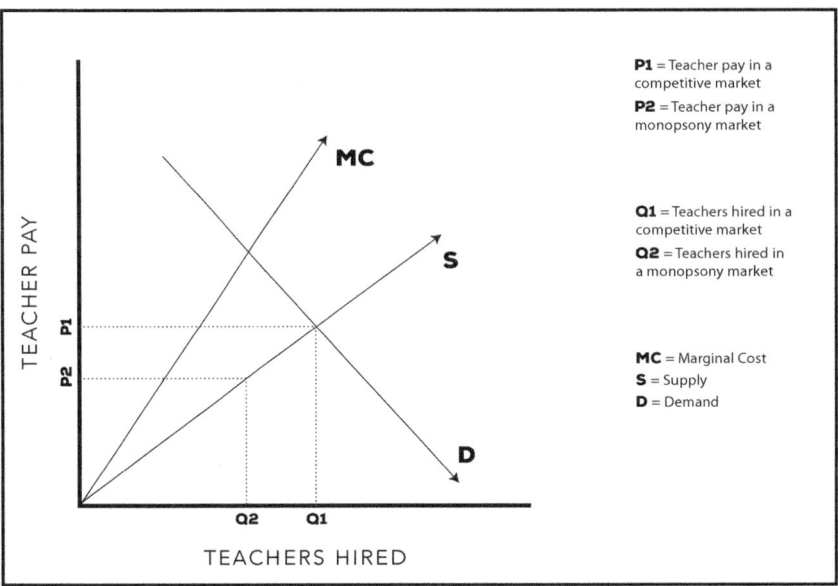

Dr. Vigdor testified, as consistent with economic theory, that providing greater choice for teachers and for parents would result in school districts being forced to pay teachers more money. In other words, the education system, as currently structured, reduces the number of teachers actually hired, and also compresses teacher pay given the monopsony power of districts.

The best way to reward teachers is not merit pay, nor the highly structured salary schedules based solely on tenure. Instead, the best solution would be to set teachers free to practice their

---

63 Jacob Vigdor, Expert testimony on 12/4/2012 in Morath v. Texas Taxpayer and Student Fairness Coalition

professions like other professionals. Once set free to practice their trade, most would earn higher and fairer pay, the profession would attract more people, and job satisfaction would increase. See more about that concept in Chapters 6 and 7.

CHAPTER 6

Teachers as True Professionals: The Professional Teacher Act, A New/Old Concept

> Today we spend about $350,000 per classroom, yet only a small part of that goes to the teacher.

Teachers should have the opportunity to serve in a truly professional capacity similar to other professionals. Although some teachers thrive under the current system in America, others do not.

Over the past half-century education leaders and policy makers have repeatedly attempted to improve education from outside the classroom; invariably these attempts for improvement have been in the form of top-down mandates. The real solution can be found inside the classroom, by allowing teachers to actually practice their profession as professionals.

The cornerstone of an efficiently organized education system would be to actually empower teachers with the opportunity to creatively meet the needs of their individual students. Instead of being required to follow the orders and mandates from those far removed from the classroom, the goal should be to empower teachers to practice as true professionals.

So, how can this be achieved? We know that top-down reform efforts have not produced the desired result. (See Chapters 4, 8, and 9.) We also know **that it would be irresponsible to attempt to tear down and rebuild the entire system. The solution: Free teachers from within the system**. At the same time, we should also consider providing greater freedom to public schools along the lines provided to charter schools. The entire education system can be improved significantly by simply allowing individual schools the freedom to customize education to the needs of individual students.

The professional teacher concept would allow public school teachers, only after they have proven themselves to be effective, the option to go into private professional practice, with funding following the child to that private practice. Model legislation for the *Professional Teacher Act* can be found at the end of Chapter 6. Although drafted for Texas, the draft can easily be adapted to other states.

Upon implementation of the *Professional Teacher Act*, a public school teacher, or group of public school teachers, who meet certain criteria would have the option to do what doctors, lawyers, accountants, engineers, and other professionals can do: Go into private practice. Teachers, for the first time in over a century, would have the ability to truly practice their trade in a professional manner. Those professional practices would be called Professional Academies.

It would be a teacher-choice type program. Teachers could specialize in what they do best, and parents and students could determine which teacher is best suited to meet the individual needs of the child.

Just as doctors, lawyers, accountants, and engineers have property rights (that is, they can own their practices), teachers could now own their professional practices. Ownership brings with it pride and the ability to build equity. Ownership is a very powerful dynamic. However, just as a doctor, lawyer, or other professional must provide their own start-up funding in order to go into private practice, teachers who start their practices should finance their own start-ups as well. They should be required to provide proof of financial ability to sustain their Professional Academies for a full year before a professional charter would be issued to the teacher/teachers by the state.

Unlike charter schools, which receive state funding from day one, the state would incur absolutely no financial risk by allowing public school teachers to start Professional Academies. The teachers running the Professional Academy would only be reimbursed after the end of the school year.

State, federal, and local laws that would apply to Professional Academies would be limited to those laws that apply to accredited private schools. Limiting federal and state mandates will maximize the ability of teachers to establish creative programs tailored to their clients' individual needs. The Commissioner of Education would adopt rules that prohibit fraud and abuse, but otherwise teachers would be free to focus on the needs of their students rather than the whims of politicians and administrators. With teachers set free to innovate, there is no limit to the number of creative programs that might be established.

This is a new concept. However, it is not unlike the way teachers exercised their profession in the late 1800s and early 1900s.[64] Many teachers during that time period owned their educational practices, and were reimbursed with state funding.

---

64 Billy Walker, Executive Director, Texas Association of School Boards [TASB], Intent of the Framers in the Education Provisions of the Texas Constitution of 1876

In the late 1800s and early 1900s many teachers, like doctors and lawyers, owned their own private educational practices.

Over the past century we have consolidated school districts and consolidated power within schools and districts. This has resulted in less authority for teachers, and less autonomy for teachers, to the detriment of students and to the detriment of common sense decisions in the classroom. Those closest to the situation—teachers—had less and less input over what happens in the classroom as more and more rules, regulations, and guidelines were imposed upon them.

Bottom line: **Teachers participating in this new program would become their own bosses, and actually serve as true professionals, with the risks and rewards inherent therein.** Innovation would be unleashed, and creative programs would abound. Students would have the ability to follow great teachers to their academies; the teaching profession would experience better retention rates, and less burn-out; and participating teachers could potentially earn significantly higher incomes since the money now spent on excessive bureaucratic oversight would go directly to them.

As noted earlier, America's total expenditure for public education is about $350,000 per classroom of 25 students.[65] Only a small portion of that cash goes to those who actually deliver education services—the teacher. **Imagine how much more efficient the system would be if teachers could determine how to allocate those funds, as needed for their students, instead of waiting for multiple layers of bureaucrats to take their cuts first.** If the average teacher were allocated only $250,000,

---

65   Fast Facts: Expenditures, National Center for Education Statistics; https://nces.ed.gov/fastfacts/display.asp?id=66

they could pay for rent, utilities, insurance, and curricula while still potentially doubling their take home pay. Teachers would be better paid, and students would be better served.

We have no way of knowing what opportunities might become available to teachers if they were given the freedom to innovate and create new educational concepts. Amanda Ripley, author of the book *The Smartest Kids in the World: And How They Got that Way*, tells about a South Korean teacher who has an office in "a luxury sky–high-rise in Seoul," has 30 employees and earns about $4 million a year.[66]

Teachers must be set free to teach! Prior to the Civil War, some slave owners felt a moral obligation to free their slaves. An argument against such action was that the freed slaves would not be able to take care of themselves. Today many school bureaucrats think that teachers would not be able to do their jobs if set free to practice their trade as true professionals. They fail to realize that many teachers would figure out how to succeed without all the rules and regulations. Nor do they realize that those teachers who might be unable to cope on their own would have other options.

Many teachers would choose to remain in the current system, while others might explore various options. Some teachers would likely operate as sole practitioners with only one classroom and a few students.

Some, instead of converting their double garage into a den, might convert it into a classroom. Others could potentially team up with other successful teachers, just as law firms build professional practices made up of multiple attorneys who complement the strengths and talents of the other partners.

---

66   NPR interview; https://www.npr.org/templates/story/story.php?storyId=217641034

Some, instead of converting their double garage into a den, might convert it into a classroom.

Still others might create specialty options or hybrid opportunities.

It is impossible to know all the opportunities which might present themselves once creative options are allowed. For example: Some creative public school superintendents might even explore ways to work with Professional Academies. For instance, they might rent a classroom to a teacher, and thereby, in essence, reverse the entire funding dynamic.

Under the current funding construct, administrators receive funding from various levels of government. Then they determine how much to spend on support efforts and how much to send to the classroom. Conversely, under the professional teacher academy concept, the actual practitioner would be in charge of determining how much to spend on the support efforts they need and how much to retain for the classroom.

The *Professional Teacher Act* would simply provide additional potential options for both educators and students. The sky is the limit when thinking about how talented teachers might structure their practices to better serve the needs of their students.

> **I am indebted to my father for living, but to my teacher for living well.**
> —Alexander the Great

In any event, **this more efficient alternative would eliminate the need for many education establishment middlemen.** Education funding would flow with the child directly to the teacher-practitioner. There would be no problem with excessive administrative costs, there would be no ridiculous mandates on teachers, no fads and fashions imposed on the teachers. Instead, the professional teacher would be in charge. Under such a funding structure there would be no limit to the ideas that could be implemented to better serve both students and teachers.

We can empower teachers and allow them the opportunities to creatively meet the needs of their students in a more professional manner. The professional teacher act concept would provide the opportunity for teachers who have proven themselves to be effective (by having been rated as proficient or better for three years) to set up their own professional practices with funding following the child. Teachers and parents would have a new choice. Teachers, students, and society would all benefit.

Once enacted, both participating and non-participating teachers will benefit from the professional academy concept.

Make no mistake: The professional teacher concept will not be one that will appeal to all teachers. However, if enacted, both participating teachers and non-participating teachers would actually benefit with such a program in place.

The professional teacher concept would be a win-win for the entire education profession, for their students, and for society.

Once teachers have an alternative career path, traditional schools will have a huge incentive to pay teachers more money and also significantly improve working conditions in order to encourage teacher retention. That is true because school districts would no longer have monopsony power over teachers. (See Chapter 5 for a discussion of how monopsony power effects teacher pay.)

Teachers who choose to start their own academies would benefit from such an alternative directly, while those who remain in the traditional system would also be rewarded indirectly through improved pay and working conditions at traditional schools due to increased competition for teachers in a more competitive teacher market. As some teachers start to take advantage of this new alternative, school administrators will also have an incentive to make better decisions regarding allocation of scarce resources. Such decisions might include fewer administrative staff, better working conditions, greater professional latitude, reduced administrative hassle, more or better classroom supplies, improved fringe benefits, and enhanced pay.

Some might contend that this is just another school choice, or voucher proposal. It is not. Instead this is a teacher choice program. **The Professional Teacher concept is limited only to public school teachers.** Public school teachers who have proven themselves to be effective would be the only people qualified to start, own, and operate a Professional Academy. This program simply provides a truly professional alternative for good teachers.

Some might contend that this is just another school choice, or voucher proposal. It is not.

So, how would a teacher evaluate this new alternative? In determining their direct participation in the professional teacher program, a teacher, or group of teachers, would go through an analysis of the potential upsides and downsides of such participation. They might ask themselves a number of questions including, but not limited to: Is it in my DNA to be my own boss? Am I better suited to continue working for others? Would such a decision be better for my family, my students, society? Should I consider going it alone, or working with other colleagues, if I were to establish a professional charter?

After preliminarily answering these questions in the affirmative, the next natural questions would probably be: Do I have the funding necessary to start an Academy and run it for a full year? If not, how could funding be obtained? What about facilities? Where would I house my classroom or classrooms?

All professionals are faced with these questions when they decide to go into private practice. However, the more qualified the individual professional, the easier it is to resolve these issues. Some will naturally go to relatives for start-up funding, others may go to a bank or venture capitalist. For example, small businesses often factor their accounts receivable so that they have the cash flow necessary to keep the doors open. ("Factoring" is the process of borrowing against future collections/accounts receivable.) Likewise, professional charter academies would be paid to after the end of the school year. This is only one of many funding options which might be available to qualified educators, however, as teachers would actually have a significant funding advantage over other professionals attempting to go into private practice.

Such financial advantages over other professionals would accrue for one colossal reason: Society values education and will do exceptional things to help enhance it. Billions of dollars are donated with the intent to help improve education. Millions of American businesses donate to education every year. Thousands of foundations donate to education year after year.

In 2014, according to IRS records, there were over 16,000 school-supporting non-profit organizations contributing to public schools. Additionally, there are many major donors to education such as the Gates Foundation, Annenberg Foundation, Walton Foundation, Target, and many others. The Gates Foundation alone has spent over $3 billion searching for better ways to improve education. Also, individuals such as publisher Ted Forstmann, John Walton, Steve Jobs, and many more who have donated huge sums to various education reform strategies.

Many of these contributors have become frustrated with the lack of progress within the current structure. As David Salisbury asked: "Does private philanthropy help a school district improve? Or do private foundations throw good money after bad by enriching a failed and ineffective education system that can't easily change? Unfortunately, it is usually the latter."[67]

Steve Jobs, after donating extensive computer equipment to schools also expressed his frustration: "no amount of technology will make a dent. What's wrong with education cannot be fixed with technology," he said. "The problem is bureaucracy."[68]

The desire to provide a quality education to our youth is widespread. This does not imply that funding for professional

---

67   David Salisbury, Private Giving to Public Schools: Does it Work? Cato Institute; https://www.cato.org/publications/commentary/private-giving-public-schools-does-it-work
68   ibid

academy start-ups would be totally funded by the private sector. Instead, the point is that many leaders would be interested in providing start-up funds for qualified individuals who have exhibited success and show prospects for future success. They could potentially loan funds to new start-ups and when paid back, re-loan those funds to another start-up, thereby greatly compounding their ability to do good things in the field of education and for society.

The professional teacher concept would be an effective way to cut through the bureaucracy.

Every community has business leaders interested in helping to improve education. That is why education professionals would have a huge advantage versus other professionals who need investors for start-up funding. Someone they know, or someone who has confidence in them and their business plan, would likely consider getting them started if they have exhibited the appropriate talent and leadership. It might be that a new privately funded foundation could be established for the specific purpose of enabling talented teachers to go into private practice. It is impossible to know what additional creative funding strategies might be forthcoming once the professional teacher concept is put into practice.

Although there will never be a perfect system, one thing is certain—the Professional Teacher Act would empower teachers to teach as true professionals. Once they are set free, creative and innovative teachers would develop programs better suited to the individual needs of their students. **Once teachers are set free to teach, America would no longer rank 37th in international comparisons** because teachers and parents who actually know the needs of their own students would produce superior results compared to those produced when politicians and bureaucrats make politically driven education decisions.

Although there will never be a perfect system, one thing is certain—the Professional Teacher Act would empower teachers to teach as true professionals.

Once the money held in trust for students is allowed to follow the child, there is no limit to the creative methods by which teachers and students, with parental oversight, can work together to achieve greater results for our society. This can be realized while at the same time significantly elevating the entire teaching profession.

Once the money held in trust for students is allowed to follow the child, there is no limit to the creative methods by which teachers and students can work together to achieve greater results for our society.

As noted earlier, the professional teacher concept would allow public school teachers, after they have proven themselves to be effective, the option to go into private professional practice, with funding following the child. Model legislation for the *Professional Teacher Act* can be found below. Although drafted for Texas, the draft can easily be adapted for other states.

Potential
Draft Texas Legislation
Professional Teacher Act

By: _____   ___.B. No. _____

A BILL TO BE ENTITLED

AN ACT

relating to the establishment of a program by which teachers can practice as professionals.

BE IT ENACTED BY THE LEGISLATURE OF THE STATE OF TEXAS:

SECTION 1. Chapter 12, Education Code, is amended by adding Subchapter F to read as follows:

SUBCHAPTER F. PROFESSIONAL TEACHER ACT

Sec. 12.201. PURPOSE. The purpose of this subchapter is to give education professionals the opportunity to function independently, with property rights similar to those afforded other professionals and the rewards inherent in those rights. Further, to allow highly qualified education professionals the opportunity to innovate and create educational programs suited for the specific needs of their student clientele.

Sec. 12.202. PROFESSIONAL CHARTER ACADEMY PROGRAM.

(a) The commissioner shall establish a professional charter academy program under which eligible education professionals are authorized to create a professional charter academy in accordance with this subchapter.

(b) The commissioner shall adopt rules to administer this subchapter. The rules shall be designed to prevent financial fraud and abuse.

Sec. 12.203. ELIGIBLE EDUCATION PROFESSIONALS. (a) To be eligible to operate a professional charter academy under this subchapter, an education professional must:

(1) have at least three years of classroom teaching experience;

(2) have been rated as proficient or higher for at least three years under the evaluation system used to evaluate the professional; or

(3) have served as the principal of a school for at least three years.

(b) A professional charter academy must be operated by at least one eligible education professional and be organized in accordance with Section 301 Business Organizations Code.

Sec. 12.204. APPLICATION OF LAWS. A professional charter academy is subject only to federal and state laws applicable to schools accredited by the Texas Private School Accreditation Commission. A professional charter academy is not subject to state law applicable to charter schools authorized by law other than this subchapter.

Sec. 12.205. INITIAL FUNDING. An eligible education professional under Section 12.203 is responsible for securing initial capital to fund the first full year of operations. State funding for students enrolled in a professional academy will only be available after completion of the full school year.

Sec. 12.206. GRANTING OF CHARTER. The commissioner shall grant a charter to operate a professional charter academy to eligible professionals under Section 12.203 if the professional provides to the commissioner:

(1) a viable business plan;

(2) proof of financial ability to fund 12 months of the academy's anticipated expenses, presented in the form of a bank letter of credit or other acceptable financial guarantee; and

(3) demonstration of parental and community interest in the establishment of a professional charter academy.

Sec. 12.207. PUBLIC FUNDING. (a) For each school year, the commissioner shall provide to a student who will attend a professional charter academy an amount equal to the average state funding, per student enrolled, received by open-enrollment charter schools during the preceding school year. The student or the student's parent may assign the funding received under this section to the professional charter academy the student attends. The commissioner may adjust the amount provided in accordance with the student's actual time actively enrolled in the program.

(b) The commissioner shall provide Chapter 48 funding to the benefit of the student's individualized education fund, or, if the funding has been assigned to the professional charter academy, to the professional charter academy not later than the 90th day after the commissioner receives enrollment data reports from the professional charter academy after the end of the school year to which funding is eligible.

(c) Federal funds and money from the available school fund may not be used to make payments under this subchapter.

Sec. 12.208. REPORTS. (a) Not later than October 1 of each year, the commissioner shall calculate the estimated number of students who are likely to attend each professional charter academy authorized under this subchapter. The report must indicate the school district a student attending a professional charter academy is eligible to attend.

(b) Not later than March 1 of each year, the commissioner shall provide actual numbers of students who attend each professional charter academy.

(c) The agency shall modify estimates of funding under Section 42.253 using the information reported under this section.

SECTION 2. As soon as possible but not later than the 45th day after the effective date of this Act the commissioner of education shall establish the professional charter academy program as required under Subchapter F, Chapter 12, Education Code, as added by this Act.

SECTION 3. This Act takes effect immediately if it receives a vote of two-thirds of all the members elected to each house, as provided by Section 39, Article III, Texas Constitution. If this Act does not receive the vote necessary for immediate effect, this Act takes effect September 1, 2020.

CHAPTER 7

Money Matters: How Money Flows is Critical

> I love money. I love everything about it. I bought some pretty good stuff. Got me a $300 pair of socks. Got a fur sink. An electric dog polisher. A gasoline powered turtleneck sweater. And, of course, I bought some dumb stuff, too.
>
> —Steve Martin

Steve Martin was joking, but he got it right. Most people agree that a lot of money is a good thing, but if it's wasted on stuff that serves no purpose, it's like having no money at all. **Everyone also agrees that the amount of money dedicated to education is important; however, how that money flows is just as critical, if not more so.** The focus must shift. Funding mechanisms must be student-based (i.e., adequacy and equity must be for students, not just for schools).

Over the past four decades, due to litigation efforts and public pressure, governors and legislators in many states have attempted to solve the school finance quandary. Many courts have ruled that schools were not adequately or equitably funded. During a large portion state leaders' tenures, many school systems were under judicial review for systemic funding faults, as determined by the courts. Many states had input from select committees, and many states implemented thoughtful reforms. However, the problems with school finance continue to haunt states throughout the nation.

Unfortunately, school finance has historically focused on the division of the spoils of government rather than actually promoting student success. The emphasis has been adequacy and equity for school systems—how much money is contributed to districts and how that money is divided between districts.

If state policy makers hope to have greater success than their many predecessors on the education finance issue, they should consider the following three realities:

- <u>First, there is a subtle yet distinct difference between what might be best for institutions and what is best for student success.</u> Funding formulas for education must be designed accordingly.

- <u>Second, there is an inverse relationship between regulation and innovation.</u> If a teacher is told what to do at every level, that leaves little latitude for innovative teaching. Therefore, teachers and schools should be allowed greater latitude over operations and delivery of services. They should be encouraged to customize, specialize, and innovate.

- <u>Third, teachers are the backbone of the system.</u> Policy makers must give more than lip service to allowing teachers to function as professionals.

Despite all past state leadership concerns, legislative efforts, reforms, and court decisions, millions of American students are underserved, and hundreds of thousands of great teachers are underpaid and grossly underappreciated. Many more have left the profession in frustration.

Most states still have school finance systems that would be considered "Byzantine," and found lacking by 21st century standards when evaluated objectively.[69] Every state in the union is faced with the continuing dilemma of how to best finance public education. As outlined earlier, even though education spending in real dollars has quadrupled,[70] and despite the fact that we spend more than most nations,[71] we have a recurring problem. When considering the decades of past attempts to solve the problem, it should be clear that real solutions can only be found by looking outside the box.

When considering the decades of past attempts to solve the problem, it should be clear that real solutions can only be found by looking outside the box.

In recent years there has been much discussion of school choice, a proposal with significant merit as based on the research. However, choice alone will not solve the education-funding problem. The manner by which the public education system is currently funded must be transformed.

Before simply tweaking the existing school finance formulas once again, as has been the norm, the three factors listed above should be addressed:

---

69   Texas Supreme Court called the Texas school finance system "Byzantine" and "sclerotic" in its 2017 School Finance ruling.
70   The Achievement Gap Fails to Close, Eric Hanushek and Paul Peterson, Summer 2019; http://hanushek.stanford.edu/sites/default/files/publications/Hanushek%20et%20al.%202019%20EdNext%2019%283%29.pdf
71   Organisation for Economic Co-operation and Development, Education at a Glance, 2019; https://data.oecd.org/eduresource/education-spending.htm

To the first point: <u>There is a subtle yet distinct difference between what might be best for institutions who deliver services and what is best for the clients they are intended to serve.</u> All institutions, schools included, have institutional interests that may or may not align with the needs of their clientele. Solving "school finance" is not the same as solving "education finance." Equity and efficiency for kids requires that, first and foremost, the primary determinant must be what works best for them rather than what works best for the institution.

Solving school finance is not the same as solving education finance.

Although in some cases institutional interests may align with student interests, to assume that they always align is a huge error in logic, resulting in a gross shortchanging of students and teachers. **Solving the education finance dilemma will require that funding decisions be made based upon the consequence they will have on individual student success rather than the assumed needs of the institution.**

State funding formulas in most states are currently designed to flow money to an institution (a school district) based on the apparent "needs" of that institution. On the surface this appears logical. Schools are designed to educate kids, so funding schools appropriately should result in the best education for those children in their care. Perhaps that is true part or even most of the time. However, not only are such formulas in most states outdated and complex (only a handful of people understand how they function), the underlying premise for their design is grossly flawed.

Finance formulas are currently designed to fund the institution and are therefore determined through political pressures exerted by those who vote and who exercise political clout: School districts and their stakeholders. Children do not hire lobbyists, do not have associations to represent their interests, or experts who manipulate the formulas to their advantage.

"Education finance" formulas will inherently differ from "school finance" formulas. "School finance" formulas are designed for institutional interests whereas "education finance" formulas would be designed to make them student-centered and designed for student success. The money would follow the child and be designed for the child's individual needs.

Most states provide funding to districts based on geography and demographics as proxies for the school district's "needs." For example, more money will flow to school districts if their students meet certain criteria, such as poverty or special needs. Under current funding systems, those funds may or may not accrue to the benefit of those particular students, and may not even flow to the actual campus that educates those students.

The misalignment between institutional funding and student-needs funding has been a distinct and recurring problem for decades, especially for special needs students, and especially for students in the inner-city, which does not have the political clout of other areas. Institutional interests will always trump student interests given how the system is designed today.

However, the underlying flaw with this funding dynamic is much greater than just this obvious misalignment. An efficient system would require that institutions be funded based on production, or service delivery, not the apparent needs of the institutions. Funding institutions as based only on their perceived needs, rather than the goods or services they actually deliver, ensures inefficiency and poor resource allocation. Such a system is unfair to students, teachers, and taxpayers. Teachers are underpaid, students often underserved, and society fails to receive full value for their investment.

Funding systems that are not rational will inherently yield inadequate results. Although sometimes institutional needs align with student needs, that is not always the case. For example: The institution may "need" a new football stadium, whereas the student needs another teacher, and the teacher needs additional classroom supplies.

A resolution to this decades-old school-finance dilemma will require a shift from funding the professed needs of school districts to funding services actually delivered to individual students. An efficiently designed education funding system would allow funds to flow with the child for actual services delivered to that particular child. Designed properly, this would benefit students, teachers, taxpayers, the economy, and enrich the quality of life for all Americans.

Such a system would result in enhanced efficiency, greater parental satisfaction, and greater support for our public schools. A properly designed system would also allow parents to determine what particular services are delivered to their children.

To the second point: There exists an inverse relationship between regulation and innovation. Schools and educators must be set free to innovate and do what they do best—focus on student success. Our American education system has enormous talent in the form of millions of great educators. We have great classroom talent as well as great management talent. If set free to create superior opportunities for both themselves and their students, all students will benefit.

A student-centered funding system should work hand-in-hand with educators' freedom to educate and innovate. **Public education is one of the most highly regulated activities in America today.** State and federal rules restrict the ability of school staff to manage the affairs of schools. Politicians, rather than educators, make policy decisions and adopt rules and regulations that not only inhibit innovation and limit educational progress, they also lead to growth in administrative overhead. As noted earlier, excessive top-down regulations have led to an exponential explosion of administrative staff expansion, as compared to student growth.

All public schools should be allowed to operate more like charter schools, which enjoy much greater regulatory latitude. Top-down control stifles innovation, creativity, and productivity. The private sector provides some insight.

All public schools should be allowed to operate more like charter schools.

For much of the 20th century, many industries were highly regulated: Trucking, airlines, telephone companies, etc. However, over the past decades, each of these industries have been deregulated to some extent. Today, we have additional delivery service providers, such as UPS, Federal Express, and even Amazon, which have thrived under the more relaxed regulatory environment. Airlines are much more competitive than before deregulation. Airlines compete with each other in both pricing and services, something they could not do when rates were set by regulation. Consumers have benefited in each instance. Before 1977 you could not own a telephone; you had to lease it from the telephone company. That change was a small step, but it opened the door to many new ideas developed by new providers who designed new and better phones.

Once set free to innovate, each industry exploded with new ideas. No one can honestly believe that if AT&T still had a monopoly over telephone services that we would have the smart phones of today. Nor would we have the cheap airfares or package delivery service we enjoy today. In each case, the establishment would have resisted change and failed to reward innovation. Great people always worked in each industry, yet the regulatory structure restricted competition and hampered innovation and progress. Institutional interests, as expressed by political power, trumped consumer interest.

What could be achieved in education if educators were really set free to practice their profession? No one can truly know how many great things could be accomplished.

On-site educators, in cooperation with parents, know what is best for the students in their care. They should be allowed to operate without excessive top-down constraint. Teachers should be set free.

Public schools should be deregulated as well. They should also be set free. They should be allowed to customize, specialize, and even franchise their innovative successes. Public schools that develop outstanding programs should be allowed to offer those services to students outside of their district lines. Public schools should be allowed to compete with charter schools. All school districts should be allowed to open their own open-enrollment charter schools wherever parents might desire their services, whether inside or outside their district boundaries.

Public schools should be allowed to aggressively compete to meet the needs of all students without regard to geography. Today, we expect each school to be all things to all students who reside in their geographic area. Education by zip code does not make a lot of sense; nevertheless, that is what we have.

Schools should be encouraged to customize and specialize when appropriate. If a school has an outstanding language, science, or other special program, those great services should not be restricted to students who reside within its boundaries. Therefore, students would have more choices regarding provision of the best services for their needs.

To the third point: Teachers are the backbone of the system; therefore, politicians must actually professionalize the education profession. Politicians give a lot of lip service to educators being professionals; however, teachers are not treated, nor rewarded, like other professionals. Policy makers must create an environment whereby educators are truly permitted to serve as professionals and receive the respect and compensation they deserve.

Teachers are the backbone of the education system. The system should be reorganized accordingly.

Education loses vast classroom talent each and every year. If a great teacher needs to earn more income, they have only two choices: They can leave the classroom and go into school administration, or they can leave the profession entirely. In either case, students lose.

Doctors, lawyers, accountants, engineers, and other professionals can all go into private practice. Such opportunities are not available to most teachers. States should consider adopting professional teacher legislation whereby teachers could go into private practice like other professionals. A sample Professional Teacher Act concept is discussed in Chapter 6.

Although this situation is not unique to Texas, in its 2016 education finance ruling, the Texas Supreme Court said that Texas students "deserve transformational, top-to-bottom reforms that amount to more than Band-Aid on top of Band-Aid. They deserve a revamped, non-sclerotic system fit for the 21st century." (Sclerotic: Becoming rigid and unresponsive; losing the ability to adapt.)

Throughout America our school systems have become very resistant to change. It is hard for these huge institutions to adapt to changing times and to changing student needs. This can be seen in the enormous number of high school graduates who must be remediated once entering college, in the thousands of teachers who leave the system due to frustration, in the high student drop-out rates, and in the thousands of kids who are grossly underserved by inner-city schools.

Policy makers around the country should follow the Texas Court's counsel and provide a 21st century education finance system for their students. Americans have enormous underutilized talent in the education community. That talent should be unbridled and funded appropriately to maximize their professional success and, as a result, superior student success.

About half of the teachers who leave the profession do so because of dissatisfaction.[72] As one teacher said upon leaving: "I

---

72   "We Aren't Seen as Professional," NEA Today, October 25, 2017; http://neatoday.org/2017/10/25/why-i-quit-teaching/

learned quickly that as a teacher, one must be resourceful and able to figure out every aspect of the job on their own. There is no relying on district administration, who often can't be bothered or are outright hostile toward teacher inquiries. We aren't seen as professionals."[73]

---

73 ibid

CHAPTER 8

Education Reform

> It is easier to put a man on the moon than to reform public schools.
>
> —Jerrold Zachiarias,
> Atomic Physicist, 1966

Attempts to reform public education have been front and center in our public debate for well over half a century. Everyone wants great public schools. And these reforms have been attempted at the local, state, and federal levels.

At the local level, a new school superintendent will often offer a new agenda for the district upon taking the job. Some are more successful than others, but often the superintendent moves on to another job and another takes his/her place, offering up still another new outline for success. At the state level, governors invariably offer up education reform plans. Attempts to improve public education continue to be very popular political issues.

At the academic level, professors in the schools of education may test a new idea and find success with a small sample of students, then promote that plan. Unfortunately, many of these ideas, whether political or academic in nature, do not work when applied to the overall system, or when tested over time. **Teachers are often frustrated by a system that requires them**

to jump from one fad to another based on directives from above in a "never-ending quest for quick, easy fixes to solve the problems of a system that has produced few notable results for more than 30 years (National Center for Education Statistics, 2013)."[74]

In the four decades between when I started teaching English at T.C. (Williams High School in Alexandria, Virginia) in 1970 and my retirement this year, I saw countless reforms come and go; some even returned years later disguised in new education lingo.
– Patrick Welsh, *Washington Post*, Sept. 27, 2013

Virtually every reform effort (local, state, or federal) has, over the decades, been designed as a top-down mandate imposed on teachers and schools. Invariably, in an attempt to improve the system from above, politicians attempt to mandate what teachers, schools, or school districts must do. Although there are hundreds of thousands of dedicated, hard-working educators in the system, little attention has been given to promoting bottom-up reforms that might set educators free to do their jobs.

The state and federal reform mandates are often bitter pills for educators to swallow. Therefore, these reforms are almost always accompanied by significant increases in funding. Consequently, funding for public education has increased by 400% over the past half-century, adjusted for inflation.[75]

---

74 "What is the impact of reform efforts over time?" The Wing Institute; https://www.winginstitute.org/what-is-impact-of853
75 The Achievement Gap Fails to Close, Eric Hanushek and Paul Peterson, Summer 2019; http://hanushek.stanford.edu/sites/default/files/publications/Hanushek%20et%20al.%202019%20

However, as indicated earlier, much of that additional funding has not made its way to the classroom.

The system is structured in a very top-down, hierarchical manner; therefore, it is natural that the solutions offered are also top-down in nature. However, a meaningful solution will require greater teacher control and teacher input. **The solutions can only be found from within the system and from within the classroom.**

For centuries, man tried to fly like a bird. Finally, once they gave up on flapping their arms like wings, we learned how to fly. Policy makers must stop flapping their arms and stop chasing fads and actually empower teachers to do their jobs. As President Bill Clinton explained, "It's the economy, stupid." In public education, "It's the structure, stupid."

There is no magic bullet. Educational success is hard work—no fad will suffice. For decades, American reformers have tried in vain to reform public education. The silver bullet will be the teacher—setting teachers free to do their jobs.

EdNext%2019%283%29.pdf

We can make an analogy in the difference between microeconomics and macroeconomics. Attempting to understand the macro economy is impossible without first understanding how individual (micro) decisions are made. Education is one-on-one, or one-with-one (one teacher with one student). Education is about the individual student, first and foremost; and then the individual teacher. If it does not work for both the teacher and the student, it does not work.

The silver bullet will be the teacher—setting teachers free to do their jobs.

All past reform attempts have focused on the school, and the system. The focus must be on the teacher and the student. As one reformer put it, the results of doing what we have been doing has resulted in **"A century of faddish ideas, but little real progress."**[76] Billions of dollars have been spent over the decades on various fads and reforms with "little real progress."

Historians see the modern education reform movement as having many faces that shift over time. The *Excellence Era* began in the early 1980s with the *Nation at Risk Report,* which called for higher high school graduation requirements, more rigorous and measurable standards, more time for student learning, better teacher preparation, and more money for schools.[77] During the *Intensification Period,* reformers built upon those same

---

76   Diana Senechal, The Most Daring Education Reform of All, American Federation of Teachers, *American Educator,* Spring 2010; https://www.aft.org/sites/default/files/periodicals/ae_spring2010.pdf

77   Jacob E. Adams, Education Reform -Overview, Reports of Historical Significance; https://education.stateuniversity.com/pages/1944/Education-Reform.html

ideals by strengthening existing rules and regulations, setting higher standards, and implementing skills tests for teachers.[78]

During the *Restructuring Period*, or *Governance Period* (late 80s to early 90s), the focus of school reform was on how schools were organized and governed. Ideas such as whole-school designs, school-based management, site-based management, and even school choice were actively advocated.[79]

In the 1980s, *Litigation* became a focus in the education arena. Although reform efforts were accompanied with additional funding, the school communities around the nation began to file lawsuits demanding even more money: Adequate, and more equitable, funding to meet the increased demands on the system.[80] Over the next 30 years all but a handful of states were forced to defend themselves at the courthouse.[81]

The *Standards Period* (1992 and forward) focused on alignments among curricula, curriculum standards, testing, and accountability systems. New reporting systems were adopted, high-stakes testing was put into place, and, in some instances, incentives and sanctions were implemented into the system.[82] This was very much a business approach to education reform: Align curricula, standards, and testing to assure adequate production.

---

78 ibid
79 ibid
80 ibid
81 Adrienne Lu, States sued over education funding, USA Today, Feb. 18, 2014; https://www.usatoday.com/story/news/nation/2014/02/18/stateline-states-education-funding-court/5577453/
82 Jacob E. Adams, Education Reform -Overview, Reports of Historical Significance; https://education.stateuniversity.com/pages/1944/Education-Reform.html

"At the state level, all states developed tests to measure student performance, and forty-nine states developed academic standards. Twenty-seven states began to hold schools accountable for results, promoting performance-based accountability but also inspiring debates about the scope and quality of standards, the adequacy of tests, and needed supports for change."[83]

These "transitions signaled the continued search for a sound theory of education reform." However, **in contrast to the level of reform activity, academic performance remained essentially flat."**[84]

Just a few of the many education reform, improvement efforts, movements, and fads imposed on educators over recent decades include:

- Common Core Movement
- Open Classroom Movement
- Block Scheduling Movement
- Adequacy and Equity: more money
- New American School Movement
- High Stakes Testing
- Standards/Accountability Movement
- Curriculum/Alignment Movement
- Governance Reform Movement
- No Child Left Behind
- Accelerated Schools
- The Edison Project
- Outcome Based Education
- Class Size
- Character Education
- Charter Schools
- Public School Choice, and Vouchers
- Merit Pay
- District Consolidation
- Constructivism Learning
- Cooperative Learning
- Core Knowledge
- Critical Thinking Movement

---

83 ibid
84 ibid

- Cultural Literacy
- Inquiry-Based Teaching
- Integrated Curriculum
- Comprehensive School Reform (CSR)
- Coalition of Essential Schools
- Ebonics
- Multiculturalism
- Phonics vs. Whole Language
- Portfolio-Based Assessments
- Principal Training
- Problem Solving
- Restructuring Movement
- School-Based Management
- School-to-Work Movement
- Self-Esteem Movement
- Socratic Method
- Success for All
- Teacher Evaluation/Quality
- In-Service Training
- Teacher Compensation
- Thematic Curriculum

With the exception of charters and choice, most of these reform efforts are top-down attempts to impose methods, procedures, or mandates on teachers and upon schools, telling them how to conduct their business. **The real solution lies within.** True reform will only occur when we empower teachers to teach, provide greater latitude for innovation, and encourage/allow greater individualized instruction.

A century of faddish ideas, but little real progress.
– Diana Senechal

As a society, we must allow for and pursue a new paradigm for success. In Chapter 6 of this book, a potential strategy is discussed that would put teachers in control, encourage greater innovation, allow teachers to function as true professionals, and also allow them to benefit personally and professionally from their success.

Education Reform Efforts in Texas, 1980–2020

Education reform has been a top priority for Texas parents, business leaders, and politicians for many decades. So, what have Texas state political leaders said and done in recent decades regarding education?

The reform sets out to change School but in the end School changes the reform.
– David Tyack and Larry Cuban

As noted previously, education policy is currently entirely driven by politics. The following discussion will show what these political decisions and actions have looked like over the tenures of six governors (in four decades) in Texas. Each governor was sincerely dedicated to education reform, and each indicated a sincere desire to improve the system.

Similar reviews could be done for every state, with similar resulting observations: Lots of desire for reform, much resistance to change, some progress, and significant backsliding over time. The education system is protective of the system itself and is very resistant to meaningful change.

One way to ascertain governors' priorities regarding their education agendas is to review their *State of the State* addresses to the legislature. Over four decades, each of the last six governors has proposed reforms intended to fix the problems of public education.

All six governors spoke to education finance, and each supported the addition of billions of dollars in new money for public education. In their respective *State of the State* speeches, all six governors supported reform or improvements in teacher training. Five governors proposed greater local control, five proposed changes to the school accountability system, five promoted a greater focus on educational basics, and five proposed raising teacher pay. Four indicated support for incentive pay programs for educators. Three governors specifically called for an end to social promotion, and two proposed significant expansion of Pre-K programs.

Only one, Governor Greg Abbott, called for significant systemic restructuring: "We're living in the 21st century while insisting on an education architecture built for the 1800s.... It's time to construct an entirely new system." Governor Abbott echoed a ruling by the State Supreme Court saying the current system is "Byzantine" and requires "transformational" change.

Why would a different approach be needed? To answer this question, let us review the status of these various reform efforts over the past four decades. Not surprisingly, governors, like most politicians, tend to identify problems to solve early in their tenures and claim victory in their later years.

In the 1979 and 1981 legislative sessions, Governor Bill Clements proposed ending social promotion, discipline reform, and a return to the basics—"reading, writing, and arithmetic." At the end of his second term, he explained that, in his first term, the Texas Legislature had passed "the most comprehensive changes to our public schools in 30 years...the back-to-basics curriculum bill, classroom discipline measures, and curtailing social promotions."

Governor Mark White was one of the most aggressive education reformers. In his special session speech in 1984 he said, "[W]e must find better ways of educating our children.... **The failures of the current system have been spelled out over and over again**. The evidence surrounds us, not just in numerous reports and studies, but in the more obvious signs of wasted human potential..... We all recognize that we face a crisis in American education...."

HB72, the act promoted by Gov. White's Select Committee which was chaired by H. Ross Perot, was passed and included many significant comprehensive reforms intended to solve the crisis. HB72 provided the first state teacher incentive program in Texas history, called the Career Ladder. It implemented a performance pay system whereby teachers could earn pay increases by working their way up that ladder. It also provided for testing teachers to evaluate their academic knowledge. It was supposed to end social promotion, reduce class size, return schools to a focus on the basics, and restructure the State Board of Education by appointing the board rather than electing it. HB72 also provided significantly more, and more equalized, funding for public education.

In 1985, Governor Mark White declared victory. He said that Texas had committed itself to **the "finest system of public education" in the nation.** He called it one of the "premier pieces of education reform in the nation." And he said that "Texans 50 or 100 years from now will realize the importance of what we did." Victory!

However, fewer than 40 years later, few of those revolutionary HB72 reforms remain in place.

Victory? Most of the HB72 reforms were undone in subsequent legislative sessions. The attempt to evaluate and reward teachers resulted in significant blowback and contributed to Governor White's defeat in the next election. The only key HB72 reforms still in place are class size reductions, additional funding, and the restructure of a few funding formula elements. One step forward and two steps back....

In 1987, Governor Bill Clements returned to the Governor's Mansion after defeating Governor White. In his 1987 *State of the State Address,* Governor Clements called for elimination of the Career Ladder and finding a better way to "reward our best teachers." He also called for elimination of teacher subject matter testing, modification of the no-pass/no-play law, and return of local control. He called for changing the "way we spend" education dollars and to "emphasize educational excellence."

In 1989, Governor Clements promoted and successfully passed "financial awards to school districts that show measurable improvement in student performance." However, that incentive system was systematically undermined and undone in subsequent years. Additionally, his plan significantly reformed the state school accountability system, but it was systematically unraveled over subsequent years. Victory?

In 1991, the top priority for Governor Ann Richards was a teacher pay increase. Although she was another proponent of local control, she declared that local control was a "hoax," that the state had "usurped" power from local boards "years ago," and turned "local educators into Austin-controlled robots." She promised to **"strip TEA** [Texas Education Agency] **policies down to the bare necessities."** She called for scrapping the Career Ladder and replacing it with mandated minimum teacher salaries, automatic cost-of-living increases, and teacher health insurance.

She was right; the state had usurped enormous power from local officials. However, that remained the case when she left office.

The most important thing Governor Richards actually accomplished was the appointment of a reform-minded Commissioner of Education: Commissioner Skip Meno. After another court ruling and six special sessions, in 1993, Governor Richards' first priority was "keeping our schools open." She also declared victory, claiming "Local control is a reality." That claim can only be viewed a political fiction.

Governor George W. Bush was another education reform governor and was very hands-on regarding education during his first legislative session in 1995. Like all his recent predecessors, he called for local control. The centerpiece of his local control agenda was the concept of Home Rule School Districts. He wanted a "stable and open" accountability system that would focus on the basic "four core subjects—math, English, science, and social science." He also requested passage of zero-tolerance classroom discipline policies and the creation of alternative schools for problem students.

Of note, since 1995, when the Home Rule School District provision was passed into law, not one Home Rule District has ever been created. Not much of a victory on that front, but he did accomplish passing charter school and other significant reforms, including a complete rewrite of the education code (for which Governor Richards should get part credit since she proposed and supported a sunset of the entire education code during the prior legislative session). The effective date for that sunset took effect in the Bush's first legislative session, so the entire *Education Code* had to be reenacted.

Included in the 1995 reform package was a provision for the creation of charter schools—a significant reform. Also imbedded in the bill was a second attempt at incentive pay—a program providing for incentive bonuses to be paid to school principals based on superior student performance at their campuses. The incentive program was never implemented by the Texas Education Agency and was removed from the *Education Code* in the subsequent legislative session. The education establishment has always been very resistant to incentives based on performance.

In 1997, Governor Bush declared, **"[W]e do face one crisis: too many of our children cannot read.** One in five is failing our reading tests...." He requested funding and legislation to establish reading academies. He also proposed a business tax dedicated to education funding, and "dedicating all the proceeds from the lottery to the school trust."

In 1999, Governor Bush declared victory: "We are already leading the nation in improving our schools by insisting on local control, high standards, and strong accountability." However, in his view, Texas still needed to "end the failed practice of social promotion." He suggested that Texas needed to spend $1 billion for teacher pay raises, to fund teacher training, and to implement a master reading teacher program. He also asked the legislature to double the $3 billion bond program for school construction. Lastly, he called for a "pilot voucher program."

The money was spent. However, many of the reforms are missing. Today, local control is still the same "hoax" Governor Richards declared it to be. Social promotion is alive and well, and most of the state's accountability system has been unraveled.

In 2001, Governor Rick Perry proposed a laundry list of reforms: $100 million for teacher training and staff development to improve early childhood literacy; $40 million for a new math initiative; a $5,000 annual bonus for Master Math Teachers; a new technology allotment of $35 per student; a tripling of the funding for a tuition program for future teachers; and $700 million for additional teacher compensation.

Although his four predecessors had long since declared victory on the issue, in 2003 Governor Perry also called for "local control." He asked for lawsuit protection for teachers, reimbursements to teachers for classroom supplies, implementation of a new science initiative, the end of the "Robin Hood" school funding system whereby property rich school districts send money to the state for redistribution to other poorer districts, and for school choice. Robin Hood is alive and well in Texas, and no new education choice programs have been passed since charters were enacted in 1995.

Governor Perry's 2005 reform agenda was more aggressive. He noted that 36,000 students were trapped in failing schools and that 889,000 students had failed the TAKS test: Texas' attempt to measure what students have learned. He called for $7,500 of incentive pay for the best teachers, end-of-course exams, the end of Robin Hood, shutting down failing public schools, expansion of teacher mentoring, increased funding for early start program, transparency in spending, and for school choice.

In 2006, significant financial and other reforms were passed into law, with billions of new dollars appropriated to education, including a $2,500 teacher pay increase. The new money was provided by enactment of a new business tax. **Two of the most substantial non-finance reforms were mandatory "end-of-course exams," and "the largest performance pay program in the nation."**

Both of Perry's major reforms, the merit pay program, and the end-of-course exams, were undone in future legislative sessions. As with past reform efforts, the new money stayed in the system and meaningful reforms disappeared over time. Victory?

In 2007, Governor Perry asked the legislature to consider a youth fitness regime in the schools, a $2,000 teacher pay increase, the ability to fire poor-performing teachers, and $80 million for early childhood education. In 2009, he asked for greater use of technology. In 2011, Governor Perry called for the expansion of the Virtual School Network and extension of STEM academies.

In 2013, Governor Perry declared victory. "We've worked hard to improve our public education system over the past decade, and the results are encouraging." However, he said; "we can't let up now." He called for more charter schools and for "scholarship programs that give students a choice," especially those locked in low-performing schools. Due to opposition from the education establishment, neither objective was achieved.

In 2015, newly elected Governor Greg Abbott echoed the goal of prior governors that we should "ensure all students are performing at grade level in reading and math by the time they finish the third grade." To achieve that elusive goal, he proposed his "high quality pre-K program." Additionally, **he called for local control by "getting rid of the one-size-fits-all mandates"** and allowing districts to "opt out of parts of the Education Code."

Unlike all his predecessors, in 2017, Governor Abbott called for systemic changes to the system. He said, **"It is time to construct an entirely new system. With a sense of urgency, we must create better ways to fund education. But school finance is not about financing our schools…. It's about providing our kids with the best education possible."**

In his 2017 address, Governor Abbott quoted James Madison, saying, "[A] well-instructed people can be permanently a free people." Abbott said the goal in educating our children is "ensuring their perpetual freedom." As noted above, he also made a plea for systemic reform. Here is the entire text of his plea for systemic change:

> But we have to realize we are living in the 21st century while insisting on an education architecture built for the 1800s. Both the house and the senate are right to tackle the vexing challenge of school finance now rather than putting it off. I agree. It's time to construct an entirely new system. With a sense of urgency, we must create better ways to fund

education. But school finance is not about financing our schools, nor is it about lining the pockets of the lawyers and lobbyists who capitalize off the backs of our students. It is about providing our kids with the best education possible. We can try to flood money to every school in an attempt to meet the needs of every student, or we could more efficiently empower parents to choose the school that best fits their child's needs. When it comes to education, we need to remember that one size doesn't fit all. What fits Dan may not fit Joe. Parents, not government, are best positioned to make decisions about their child's education. Parents should be empowered to choose the school that's best for their child. Senator Taylor, I agree: No child should be in the wrong school because of their zip code. Every child should have a chance to succeed in life. And yes, Representative Simmons, every child should have the ability to attend the school that's best for them. Thirty states have school choice. Let's make Texas the 31st.

In 2019, Governor Abbott noted that although we are graduating more students from high school, less than 40% of those who take the ACT or SAT test are actually ready for college and that only 40% of third graders can actually read at the third grade level. He indicated that the state should recruit and retain the "best and brightest teachers" and should find ways to allow the "best teachers to earn a six-figure salary." He therefore declared education finance reform and teacher pay as emergency items for the legislative session.

It is too early to evaluate the long-term impact of Governor Abbott's efforts. However, looking back through history, one thing is evident: The current public education system is very resistant to meaningful change.

Larry Cuban and David Tyack were correct when they said, "The reform sets out to change School, but in the end School changes the reform.[85]"

The reform sets out to change School, but in the end School changes the reform.
– Larry Cuban, David Tyack

A Quick Review of Top-Down Reform Results:

- Every past attempt to inject **incentives or merit pay** programs into the system has been reversed over time.
- **Strong accountability measures** inevitably get watered down over time.
- Today, as Ann Richards said in 1991, real **local control remains a "hoax."**
- **Social promotion** remains a consistent problem despite the numerous victories declared over it.
- **The achievement gap** remains at unacceptable levels.
- The only school reform guaranteed to survive is **more money.**

Each of these issues—merit pay, accountability, ending social promotion, as well as many others—are attempts to mandate change from above. Of course, greater "local control' is actually just the opposite—it is the attempt to remove mandates from above. In almost all reform efforts, the attempted or proposed solution was to make change happen from above. Although all were well intended, there is a big difference between a good idea and an idea that will work in actual practice.

---

85 David Tyack and Larry Cuban, *Tinkering Towards Utopia: A Century of Public School Reform*

Although virtually everyone gives lip service to local control, the incentives built into the current system make achievement of local control impossible. Bureaucrats and politicians adopt rules in an attempt to solve problems. The general mindset is that every problem has a potential legislative or regulatory solution; therefore, new rules and regulations will be enacted and unintended consequences will inevitably follow.

There is a big difference between a good idea and an idea that will work in actual practice.

The rulebook will always continue to grow, and the common sense of the teacher will be trumped by rules and regulations from above. So much for local control, and so much for teacher control as long as the system remains as currently structured. Approaches must be considered that will allow teachers to practice their profession in a truly professional manner.

Four decades ago, Governor Mark White said, "[W]e face a crisis in American education." More recently, Governor Greg Abbott said, "We're living in the 21st century while insisting on an education architecture built for the 1800s.... It's time to construct an entirely new system."

We still "face a crisis in American education," which Governor White identified back in 1985, and we will continue to do so until we take a new path outside the confines of the autocratic scheme in place today, as suggested by Governor Abbott in his call to "construct an entirely new system."

We still "face a crisis in American education," which Governor White identified back in 1985.

Sadly, there are many examples of hard-fought-for education reforms that have been undone over time due to political forces. Key business leaders spent decades promoting reform efforts designed to improve education in Texas. Leaders like Ross Perot, Charles Miller, Sandy Kress, Rod Page, Woody Hunt, Tom Luce, Bill Hammond, Jim Windham, Don McAdams, and hundreds of other business leaders working individually or through organizations such as the Texas Association of Business, and the Texas Business Leadership Council (formally known as the Governor's Business Council), spent significant time, effort, and money in attempts to improve education in Texas. They made progress; however, in subsequent legislative sessions, each reform measure was undone piece by piece due to political pressure from the education community. Each reform effort was accompanied by more money; over time the money stayed and the reforms either went away or were watered down significantly.

What can we learn from these past education reform efforts? It is always easy to say, "this time we will do it right." However, as Einstein said, the definition of insanity is doing the same thing and expecting a different result. A real solution will require an examination of the underlying problem.

Too often we confuse logic with politics. Just because something seems logical does not mean it will work politically. Political power will always trump what would be logical in a non-politically driven system. It is a fool's errand to attempt to inject artificial market dynamics into a top-down politically driven system.

A system driven totally by political power will unfortunately always be inefficient, inequitable, and wasteful.

Too often we confuse logic with politics. A system driven totally by political power will always be inefficient, inequitable, and wasteful.

CHAPTER 9

The Achievement Gap Can Be Closed

> Closing achievement gaps is more urgent today than ever before, and dramatic success is possible. Academic excellence is difficult to achieve, but is not a controversial goal.
>
> —Ronald Ferguson, in *Toward Excellence with Equity*

One of the gravest problems facing the nation in education today is the unacceptable gap in achievement levels of minority students. Closing the achievement gap will require a complete reevaluation of how we view educational funding. In a perfect world, every dollar put into the education system would be used to benefit students. But too often we view school funds simplistically as belonging to a school district. In fact, they actually belong to taxpayers and are held in trust for students—that is why school board members are called trustees. Teachers, parents, and students must be empowered to use those trust funds in the manners best suited to the individual needs of each and every student.

Closing the gap will require:

- Allowing a natural transformation of education into the 21st century;
- Funding education rather than funding the process of schooling;

- Funding strategies which benefit both students and providers;
- Relaxation of rigid regulation of the school industry;
- Setting teachers free to address the needs of individual students;
- Education providers funded for the services they actually provide, rather than as artificial proxies for institutional needs;
- Relaxation of monopolistic control over students and taxpayers based solely on geographic restrictions;
- Ceasing to finance schools for warehousing kids. (Schools are funded based on student attendance, and student characteristics, not the services actually provided.)

The National Assessment of Education Progress (NAEP) indicates a stagnation of academic results across the nation. For example, although in 2000 George W. Bush ran for president in part on the "Texas Miracle" in education,[86] NAEP results for 2019 indicate Texas is actually losing ground. Eighth grade math scores peaked in 2011, with 40% rated as proficient or better, compared to only 29.5% in 2019. Reading for 8th graders peaked in 2013, with 30.8% proficient or better compared to only 25% in 2019. Further, the Texas black-white achievement gap was 28 points, and the Hispanic-white achievement gap was 20 points in 2019.[87] **Critically, the achievement gap**

---

[86] CBS News, *60 Minutes*; https://www.cbsnews.com/news/the-texas-miracle/

[87] The Nation's Report Card; https://www.nationsreportcard.gov/profiles/stateprofile/overview/TX?cti=PgTab_OT&chort=2&sub=MAT&sj=TX&fs=Grade&st=MN&year=2019R3&sg=Race%2FEthnicity%3A+White+vs.+Hispanic&sgv=Difference&ts=Single+Year&tss=2015R3-2019R3&sfj=NP

for minority students continues to haunt the entire nation at unacceptable levels.

Over the years, many states have explored strategies intended to close the achievement gap, including reading and math initiatives, curricula modifications, professional development programs, high-stakes testing, accountability reforms, and targeted funding. None of these have solved the problem; in fact, one report indicated "experts warn against making broad conclusions for or against any specific education strategy."[88] The problem continues at unacceptable levels and, therefore, restricts success for many students.

Virtually all the reforms mentioned above were accompanied by additional spending, yet the results have been questionable at best. Money does matter. But whatever the endeavor, the

---

88   Aliyya Swaby and Ryan Murphy, "Texas education officials promise focus on math, reading after 'lagging' report card," *Texas Tribune*, April 11, 2018; https://www.texastribune.org/2018/04/11/texas-education-agency/

manner by which money flows directly impacts the results those dollars will produce. So, how do we currently fund education?

When government decides to fund a worthwhile program, it can either decide to fund the process or fund the product/result. For example, the government funds the process of running Veterans Administration hospitals, i.e., funding based on process. Through Medicare, the government funds a doctor for performing a hip replacement, i.e., funding based on product.

If farmers were paid based on the number of seeds they put into the ground, or the number of rows of cotton planted, they would be receiving funding based on process. If each farm were given a budget based on anticipated cost of running that farm and then funded accordingly, that too would be process funding. If instead, farmers were paid based on what they harvest, then funding would be based on real productivity—the result/product.

The government can purchase an airplane on a fixed-cost basis, thereby paying for result, or it can purchase an airplane on a cost-plus basis, in which case it is funding the process of manufacturing the aircraft. The difficulty is in accurately quantifying and rewarding the appropriate elements for funding. This is especially true with process-oriented funding.

With a fixed price for an explicit product, costs are straightforward and transparent. However, process-based funding is much more difficult, and much more complex, often resulting in gross inefficiencies and cost overruns due to the fact that the incentive structure is entirely different than with fixed-based funding. Process-based funding is determined by measuring inputs; product-based funding is determined by measuring outputs.

The more difficult questions for any government venture are: Do we fund based on process or product? If formulas are based on process, what are the appropriate elements to plug into the formulas? If funding is based on result, then who will determine value-added result? How do you fairly measure value-added results in any government endeavor?

In a politically driven system how do you assure objective evaluation, rather than bias in favor of those with political influence? These are tough questions and are the main reasons why school finance has become excessively complex over the decades.

Whether agriculture, finance, aerospace, medicine, government, or any other industry, how money flows impacts the industry's results. If farmers were paid based on process (number of seeds planted or some other input measure) aggregate production in the industry would definitely be diminished. If an automobile manufacturer were paid based on process, then both the cost and delivery lead-times for autos would be greater. This would be true of any enterprise which is funded by process simply because there is always something else to be done. If funds are flowing based on activity instead of what is produced, there will be more activity, whether that activity is productive or not. Funding activity/inputs rather than actual outputs will inevitably result in more activity/inputs and higher costs regardless if productivity actually increases, remains stagnant, or declines.

A top-down system will normally defer to process-oriented accountability, and funding. It will attempt to substitute market mechanisms with artificial alternatives to market value. For example, the Soviets attempted to reward the nail industry based on the number of tons of nails produced. They were attempting to inject artificial market dynamics—production based on tons of nails—into a top-down system. The natural result was a huge shortage in small nails, and a huge surplus in large nails, simply because a thousand more easily produced large nails greatly outweighed a thousand smaller nails.

Artificial measurements attempting to mirror markets rarely work. This is one reason teacher merit pay programs have failed. It is hard to determine academic results in a fair manner. Artificial measurements are always viewed as being unfair because selection of truly objective criteria is difficult, if not impossible, especially in a politically driven system.

Artificial measurements attempting to mirror markets rarely work.

Education funding is now totally process oriented. Not only that, most of the process variables and formula elements are calculated based on proxies for student needs. Funding does not actually follow the child to a campus or to a classroom. Instead, funding just goes to a larger institution, the school district, to be allocated as it determines based primarily on the political dynamics of the district. Those with political clout win; those without political clout lose.

Suppose commercial fishermen were paid based on the number of hours their nets are in the water. The result would be more time in the water, simply because they are paid based on the time spent on the task. The result would be fewer fish because funding would be based on process rather than result.

If, however, the funding formulas were based on fish harvested, then the nets might actually be in the water less because the captain would take time to move the ship to more productive waters. The result would be more fish caught. If the formula that determines funding were based on the number of fish harvested, the result would be a lot of small fish in the net, whereas if the formula were based on the pounds of fish caught, then the harvest might result in larger fish. Each and every element of any funding formula will influence actions and therefore results.

Following the fisherman analogy: Schools are not funded based on harvest (student success) because it is difficult to accurately and fairly measure the value added by the school. Schools are not even funded based on the time the fishing nets are in the water. Instead, it is as if the fisherman's entire fleet were funded based on the number and characteristics of the fishing nets in the main warehouse (student demographics) instead of nets on boats and/or in the water.

A school district that does a good job of allocating and placement of nets is paid the same as a district that does a lousy job. School finance formulas do not fund school campuses or classrooms; instead, school districts are funded by the formulas. Campus funding is totally dependent on action by the district. Inner-city schools are thus often shortchanged.

Inner-city school districts often have hundreds of thousands of students. Superintendents are paid tens of millions of dollars to manage these huge districts. **No human is smart enough to micromanage a school district with 200,000 kids.** Only the captain of the ship, the teacher, with perhaps help from the fleet commander, the principal, know where and when the nets should be placed into the water so that the nets can best harvest learning from the sea of knowledge.

Education can learn from the history of commerce. Make no mistake: Education is a huge industry in America with budgets of about $700 billion annually. The industry employs millions directly (3.1 million teachers, and 3.3 million non-teachers)[89]

---

89 Dr. Benjamin Scafidi; https://www.edchoice.org/wp-content/uploads/2017/06/Back-to-the-Staffing-Surge-by-Ben-Scafidi.pdf

plus hundreds of thousands more who receive taxpayer funds indirectly, including contractors, lawyers, consultants, publishers, association employees, and others who rely on the education industry for their livelihood.

Schools are the cornerstone of the education industry. Historically, schools have provided most education services, so we fund schools as a proxy for the education process. Then we attempt to determine how much it costs to run schools—a task experts have struggled, in vain, to master for decades.

Currently, the key component for determining school funding is student attendance. The attendance number is then adjusted for certain weights. These weights are an attempt to adjust for school cost differentials due to student and community characteristics. For example, in an attempt to help close the achievement gap, most formulas provide greater funding for districts that have more poor students.

However, school districts get these extra funds regardless of their progress in closing any academic achievement gap, regardless of whether they actually use the funds for campuses that house those targeted students, regardless of the actual remedial needs of students, and regardless of whether the funds are actually used to address the remediation needs of each targeted student.

What if these remediation funds went to a campus based on actual progress in closing the achievement gap? What if teachers were set free to establish, and control, special schools focused on closing the gap? Greater progress could be made if educational providers were actually paid for progress (product) rather than process.

Funding based on the actual harvest, in lieu of just head count and seat time, would greatly benefit students and would enable us to close the achievement gap. The problem, however, is who decides how progress is measured. A top-down system is incapable of making such a determination. Instead, teachers and parents must be set free to make such determinations on their own.

Funding should follow the actual child, not some proxy for that child. Educational providers should be funded based on delivery of services to each individual student, not a proxy for perceived school needs. As an analogy for this situation, let us look at how another service, phone service, was provided and how those services changed over time.

For most of the 20th century, we paid telephone companies for phone services. The country was divided into regions and phone companies had monopoly power over these regions. All phone services, and equipment, was provided by the phone companies. Consumers paid for the *process* involved in telephone services. We basically funded telephone companies rather than paying for the product they provided.

Through deregulation, the monopoly power of these phone companies waned, and other vendors started providing different kinds of phones, and eventually the entire telecommunications industry was transformed. The service providers have totally transformed themselves, and we no longer fund telephone companies. Instead, we fund communication services. We pay for products (the phones, text, Internet, etc.) instead of paying for process (funding phone companies).

Naturally, the phone companies felt more secure with their monopolies; however, deregulation did not produce a situation that pitted consumers against producers. Instead, deregulation was a win-win. Consumers benefited immensely while the industry as a whole has grown and thrived even more.

> **Just as we adjusted from funding "telephones" to funding "communications" through the telecommunications industry, we must shift from just funding "schools" to actually funding "education" in the education industry.**

Just as we adjusted from funding "telephone providers" to funding "communications" through the telecommunications industry, we must shift from just funding "schools" to actually funding "education" in the education industry.

Today, the education community is very resistant to change, just as was the telephone industry. The education community should not be fearful. With properly structured change, teachers would earn significantly more money, have significantly more professional discretion, greater control over their classrooms, and significantly enhanced job satisfaction.

Education is not immune to transformation, except as limited by government. If we are to close the achievement gap, we must set teachers and parents free to decide what is best for the children in their charge and flow funding accordingly. See Chapter 6 for an idea of how to accomplish that objective.

Education is not immune to transformation, except as limited by government.

It is time to lead in closing the achievement gap. It can be achieved!

CHAPTER 10

Equity, Adequacy, & Litigation

> School finance is like a Russian novel, it's long, it's boring, it's complex, and in the end, everyone dies.
>
> —Mark Udof, former Chancellor; University of Texas

All Americans want a quality education for America's students. The education funding puzzle must be solved. In order to solve the puzzle, we must reevaluate the problem. What are our goals? What is in the best interest of all students? What can we learn from history? Is new funding needed? If so, how much? Is current funding equitably and appropriately allocated?

Without question, the top priority for the public education establishment as a whole has consistently been additional funding. **As of 2014, all but five states had been sued over funding for education.**[90] Litigation has proven to be an effective means by which the school establishment can demand and receive more money than politicians are voluntarily willing to provide. The litigation is usually grounded on two arguments:

---

90   Adrienne Lu, States sued over education funding, USA Today, Feb. 18, 2014; https://www.usatoday.com/story/news/nation/2014/02/18/stateline-states-education-funding-court/5577453/

First, that schools are not adequately funded, and second, that funding is not equitably distributed among school districts.

As a side note, it is odd that this litigation has involved inequity of funding for school districts, not for schools. **However, in many states, the inequity is greater among campuses within districts than among school districts.** It is interesting to note that school campuses are not independent institutions, whereas districts are; therefore, an individual campus is not in a position to litigate over funding. This is just one example of how the structure of the education system significantly effects all political, funding, and legal decisions within the system.

Equity has been a divisive issue between districts, and within the entire education establishment, as it pits the have-not districts against the haves. The adequacy issue, however, tends to unify the entire education establishment. Political decisions always seek consensus, so the education establishment always circles the wagons and universally supports the demand for more money, that is, for adequacy. Litigation over equity issues has always been more contentious. So, whether the debate occurs at the courthouse or the statehouse, the one song sung in unison from the entire education community is "We Need More Money."

The question is how much new money is enough? How much is adequate? School finance experts always attempt to quantify the actual dollars needed to efficiently deliver a quality education. **However, there is never a consensus on how much money is actually required because that number is impossible to determine.**

As any economist will tell you, the actual cost of any product or service is determined by supply and demand. Since education services are essentially delivered by a monopoly, the intersection of supply and demand can never be accurately measured.

Therefore, all attempts to estimate the cost of education must be based on spending patterns alone. So, whatever is spent by government becomes the assumed cost. If a district is run efficiently, the cost will be less; if run inefficiently, the cost will be more. (See Chapter 5 for an explanation of why this funding dynamic actually results in suppression of teacher pay.)

This is quite a puzzle to solve when, according to the experts, more money is always required, yet few taxpayers want new or higher taxes. To add to the quandary, no one can tell you how much new money is actually needed. Although it is very easy to call for more funds, it is impossible to quantify how much, which leads to the conclusion that there can never be enough.

For almost a half-century, states have been wrestling with the thorny issue of school finance and school finance litigation. Time and again, legislatures have tweaked the system, only to find themselves back at the courthouse defending the latest legislative action, or at the statehouse debating tax increases to provide more funding. The political and legal pressures have consistently been for greater funding.

At virtually every legislative hearing around the country, legislators have heard, year after year, the cries for more money. Every legislator, and every governor, has heard the chorus loud and clear. Accordingly, politicians have delivered. Significant additional funding has gone into the system; however, too little actually ends up in the classroom.

Once new funds are obtained, they are usually viewed as "down payments" on what is truly needed. What goes unsaid, though, is there is never enough money. **Economists call this concept scarcity. There is never enough of anything.** We would all love to have a nicer home, a better car, more vacations, and other things we consider valuable. The law of scarcity tells us that resources are always limited in the face of unlimited desires. These limited resources require their efficient allocation.

Regardless of revenue source or amount of increase in money allocated, the system will always easily consume those funds and will consistently ask for more. That is simply the nature of huge bureaucracies. More money may change the equation temporarily, but it does not address the basic problem—distributing the available dollars to best serve students and the teachers who serve those students. Students and teachers should be the priority. However, teachers and students are too often used as political pawns to feed the bureaucratic system.

Clearly, a different approach is required if the seemingly endless cycle of litigation, political pressure, and bureaucratic growth is to ever to subside. A solution to the puzzle will require a different approach. **Schools are funded today, in most states, through a hodgepodge of highly complex and outdated formulas that would make a nuclear physicist's head spin**, formulas which oftentimes have little relation to what is required to educate a child.

The current school funding formula systems have evolved primarily based on political considerations. In other words, politicians tweak the school funding formulas to deliver additional funding to those school districts politicians wish to favor, in order to harvest sufficient votes for passage of their preferred legislation. School finance formulas, around the country, have become a way to earmark and disguise funds for political purposes.

That is simply how the political process works. Greater complexity allows for greater political manipulation. When states decided to value differing groups of students differently, this required subjective decisions, and subjective decisions always allow for greater political manipulation. Once the concept of equal per-capita state funding per child was abandoned, the gamesmanship of earmarking for political gain was unleashed. Likewise, funding decisions based on funding for schools rather than funding for students enable even greater political manipulation.

By funding institutions rather than funding students, we encourage political abuse. Each year, around the country, billions of taxpayer dollars flow directly, or indirectly, to groups and associations representing various educational interests. These groups encourage tens of thousands of school employees, association staff, paid consultants, attorneys, lobbyists, and others to sing the "more money" song in unison. If the song is successful, taxpayers foot the bill for the song itself and for the additional spending which the song promoted.

The focus should be funding for the child rather than funding the system's establishment. Every child deserves the same educational opportunities regardless of place of residence. Funding should be based on the child's needs, not the school's perceived needs.

In 2017 Americans spent over $300,000 for a classroom of 25 children[91] while the average teacher nationwide only earned about $60,000. That represents a five-to-one ratio between value-added labor and overhead costs—a very high ratio by any rational standard. The system, as designed today, greatly undervalues the teacher-led classroom effort. If we are to prosper, this must change.

As indicated earlier, in the one-room schoolhouse, the teacher was in total control. In multi-room campuses, the principal or headmaster was in total control. However, over the decades the

---

91 U.S. Census news release May, 21, 2019; https://www.census.gov/newsroom/press-releases/2019/school-spending.html

system has grown and decision-making has moved even farther from the classroom.

Between 1940 and 2009, the number of school districts in America fell from 120,000 to about 12,000.[92] School consolidation was seen as an efficiency move due to potential economies of scale. **In hindsight, however, we see vast diseconomies of scale caused by the growth of huge bureaucracies.** Educational decisions made from afar often undervalue efforts at the classroom level, while overvaluing administrative bloat.

If we really value the classroom effort, the education funding structure must change to reflect, and fund, the value of the classroom. **Our funding system should fund students equally, be completely transparent, and be easily understood by teachers, administrators, and taxpayers.**

The priorities of the system are upside down. The money flows to the administrators; they take what they want and give what's left to the teachers in the classroom.

By funding institutions, in lieu of students, the system creates inherent inefficiencies. For example, teachers often complain that they lack adequate classroom supplies.[93] The central office, however, is rarely short of supplies and equipment. The priorities of the system are upside down. The money flows to

---

92 The Case for the One-Room School Houses, Foundation for Economic Education, August 14, 2017; https://fee.org/articles/the-case-for-one-room-school-houses/
93 Teachers Begging for Basics; https://okcfox.com/news/project-oklahoma/study-finds-local-districts-not-prioritizing-spending-for-classroom-necessities

the administrators; they take what they want and give what's left to the teachers in the classroom.

One study found that 94% of America's teachers have to purchase supplies for their classrooms out of their own pockets.[94] Another study found that Oklahoma City teachers have resorted to "begging for basics," using a website to request that businesses donate such things as copy paper, printers, ink, frogs to dissect, whiteboard supplies, dictionaries, and chairs for small children so that they can meet the needs of their students.[95] This is a common problem in many classrooms around the country while it **is doubtful that the central office is short of such supplies.**

When teachers have to go begging for basic equipment and supplies…it is obvious that politics and administrative convenience are higher priorities to those in charge.
—Dr. Byron Schlomach

The practitioners who are actually delivering the services taxpayers are paying for should have greater control over the allocation of resources needed to deliver their services. Supplies for the classroom should take priority over administrative desires, but currently they do not. Current education funding systems fail to flow dollars in a manner that maximizes the efficient allocation of scarce resources.

---

94   Niraj Chokshi, "94 Percent of U.S. Teachers Spend Their Own Money on School Supplies, Survey Finds," New York Times, May 16, 2018; https://www.nytimes.com/2018/05/16/us/teachers-school-supplies.html.
95   Teachers Begging for Basics; https://okcfox.com/news/project-oklahoma/study-finds-local-districts-not-prioritizing-spending-for-classroom-necessities

An equitable student-centered funding system would deliver not only equity for students but would also fairly reward classroom teachers. Designed appropriately, such a system would provide greater efficiency, empower both teachers and parents, enhance student performance, and limit future ligation over education funding. Money should follow the child, and the actual practitioner must have a significant say in how those dollars are used.

CHAPTER 11

Original Intent of the Texas Constitution

Article 7, Section 1. SUPPORT AND MAINTENANCE OF SYSTEM OF PUBLIC FREE SCHOOLS. A general diffusion of knowledge **being essential to the preservation of the liberties and rights of the people**, it shall be the duty of the Legislature of the State to establish and make suitable provision for the support and maintenance of an efficient system of public free schools.[96]

> Although most people think the first Texas charter schools came after the reform bill in 1995, charter schools were common in Texas long before what we now call "public" schools even came into existence.

It isn't commonly known that public free schools, as mandated by the Texas state constitution, were not originally state-run schools, but community schools. Any group of parents could form a school, hire a teacher, and seek reimbursement from the state.

Texas, like many states, has spent an enormous amount of time and money in legal and legislative debates over education funding during the past half-century. This is not new to our age, however. A similar struggle over education delivery and

---

96   Texas Constitution, Article 7, Section 1

funding existed since Texas was a part of Mexico.[97] Let us look back in time:

The Constitution of the Republic of Texas in 1836 simply required Congress to "...as soon as circumstances will permit, to provide by law a general system of education."[98] Fredrick Eby, a University of Texas professor and proponent of government-run schools, wrote the following in his 1925 education history book:

> "There is no evidence that any of these men [drafters of the Constitution] had in view a state-endowed, state-supported, and likewise state-controlled system for the training of the young."

Eby goes on to say:

> "The First Congress in 1837 was strangely silent on the subject of popular education. It concerned itself with chartering several private institutions."[99]

Although most people think the first Texas charter schools came after the reform bill in 1995, charter schools were common in Texas long before what we now call "public" schools came into existence. Although today Texans have no private school options within the "public free school" system, Texans did have such options both before and after the current *Texas Constitution* was adopted in 1876.[100] Public education, as we

---

97 "In no other state has the struggle of such diverse traditions and ideas been so prolonged and bitter." Eby, The Development of Education in Texas, 1925
98 Republic of Texas Constitution 1836
99 Eby, The Development of Education in Texas, 1925
100 Billy Walker, Executive Director TASB, *Intent of the Framers in the Education Provisions of the Texas Constitution of 1876.* "In 1876, the historical balance between private-school and public-school interests was maintained as a compromise measure, and

know it today, has evolved over decades. As Billy Walker, past executive director of the Texas Association of School Boards (TASB), said, "public education floundered in chaos for half a century after the [Civil] war."[101]

The current Texas Constitution, which was written in 1876, was the result of great debate and contention, no less so than around the issue of education.[102] In fact, there was more debate over the education issue than any other item before the convention.[103] Negative reaction to the highly centralized 'radical school system,' established by the carpetbaggers during reconstruction was the driving force for using the 1845 Constitution as a starting point when drafting a new constitution in 1875—as opposed to using the Radical Republican Constitution which was in place at the time.[104]

Given that 1845 Constitution was the basis for the 1876 rewrite, we should examine the words used in that first document. Of particular interest is the use of the two terms "public schools" and "free schools." in those debates. The first section of the Texas Constitution of 1845 imposed upon the legislature the duty of making "suitable provision for the support and maintenance of <u>public schools</u>." The second section, which follows that declaration immediately, requires that the legislature "shall, as early as practicable, establish <u>free schools</u> throughout

---

the community system was allowed to exist in some Texas counties until 1909," p.670
101 Billy Walker, Executive Director TASB, *Intent of the Framers in the Education Provisions of the Texas Constitution of 1876*, cited in *Edgewood III*, p.640
102 No subject was more controversial or more extensively debated. West Orange Decision, 2006
103 Constitutional Convention Journal, 1875
104 Constitutional Convention Debate Records, 1875

the state and shall furnish means for their support by taxations of property...."

Critical to understanding the original intent of these words is knowing that "public" did not mean government-operated schools as we think of the term today; instead it only meant schools that would be "open to the public" as might a restaurant or store that is open to the public. And "free" meant that poor students were entitled to attend regardless of ability to pay.

Billy Walker noted that "the vast majority of schools in the late 1850s were private, the education provisions operated most typically as an early voucher system with parents selecting their children's educational facilities and the state disbursing a per capita amount to the school, whether public (usually municipally controlled) or private."[105]

In the mid-1800s, Walker continued, the "idea of a general system of taxation for financing state-supported and state-operated schools still violated the thinking of most Texans, who construed 'public' schools as mentioned in the constitution, to indicate both private and community education enterprises.... Although few citizens actually supported the idea of state-financed public schools, the concept did have its proponents.... This philosophical battle explains to a large extent the vacillating course that Texas school finance followed in the nineteenth century."[106]

In 1925, Eby wrote:

> "It has been seen that the constitution required the legislature to make provision for two types of schools, 'public' and 'free'.... This particular difference is due to the fact that this

---

105   Billy Walker, Executive Director TASB, *Intent of the Framers in the Education Provisions of the Texas Constitution of 1876*, p.639
106   ibid, p.634-635

> article of the constitution was a compromise agreed upon by the various sociological groups which held quite divergent opinions as to education.... One of the methods of compromise may be seen in the plan adopted in New York of distributing state funds among the various private and denominational schools."[107]

He continues:

> "The first section of the new constitution [of 1845] required the establishment of 'public schools.' This indicated the adoption of a general policy of assisting the people in their private and community enterprises. It did not propose free tuition for all...general taxation for popular education...or a state-owned [system].... On the contrary the advocates of private and church schools fully expected the state to assist in promoting their particular enterprises.... The second section [of the 1845 Constitution] provided for 'free schools' by taxation on property. The private and church school advocates favored this policy as a wise charity for the education of the orphaned and indigent.... Tuition would be paid by the state and that they would attend the existing [private] institutions.[108]

Furthermore, back in 1925, Eby pointed out the fact that even then these two terms, "public" and "free," did not mean what they did when written in 1876: "For the first [public] no special funds are fixed; for the second [free], one tenth of the annual revenue is positively reserved."[109] So, neither constitutional provision required the government to own or operate schools, as we think of "public schools" today. Reading the constitutional language and the debates surrounding it can be confusing unless you understand the context in which these terms were used.

As written in the 1845 Constitution, the 1854 law:

---

107 Eby, *The Development of Education in Texas*, 1925
108 ibid
109 Eby, *The Development of Education in Texas*, 1925 p. 108

> "....represents the views of...three divergent types of school organizations: a system of public schools, pauper schools, and private schools enjoying the bounty and support of the state.... Throughout the entire state and with but few exceptions the people resorted to the use of private schools which under the law [1854] could be designated 'common schools....' No state system of public schools was possible under the conditions.... People soon learned that public free school meant *free* only to those who confessed themselves paupers...."[110]

> "The system as finally developed in 1858 was simple in the extreme.... Those parents who desired could form a school and could secure their own teacher and receive the state apportionment for their children. Those wishing to patronize one of the existing private schools were permitted the same privilege."[111]

So, both a "public" school system and a "free" school system could support private, or community, schools under the total control of parents.

During September and October 1875, the most contentious and highly volatile issue of constitutional debate in Austin was education. All education resolutions were sent to the education committee consisting of 15 members. This committee failed to reach consensus and sent both majority and minority reports to the floor of the convention. The full convention also failed to reach agreement, and the issue was then sent to a Select Committee of seven members. That committee also failed to reach agreement, which also issued both majority and minority reports.[112] Each time the education issue reached the floor, it attracted serious and contentious debate.

---

110   ibid
111   ibid
112   Constitutional Convention Journal, 1875

Given the friction and varying views regarding education, the word "efficient" appears to have been part of the compromise. Data on the actual constitutional debates are very limited. However, it appears that one of the greatest issues was that of taxation, if any, and how much. As will be seen, only a small minority seemed supportive of actually allowing government to control and run schools.[113]

Like the 1845 compromise, the 1876 compromise included both the "free" and "public school" language. However, in 1876, they merged the two terms into the same phrase: "…the Legislature of the State to establish and make suitable provision for the support and maintenance of an *efficient system of public free* schools."[114]

Our present Constitution produced what become known as the community school system:

> "The method of school organization adopted in the new law [of 1876] was as simple and as loose as it could possibly be.… (1) It gave to parents the greatest latitude in determining for themselves the kind of education they desired for their children and the character of teacher they wished to employ. (2) There was no restriction to the number of children necessary to constitute a school community..… (3) The parents could enjoy the use of the state school fund, together with the minimum of state interference. Moreover, it lodged the responsibility of educating the children upon the parents, where, as they believed, it belonged.…" Additionally, students were not restricted by geographic boundaries.[115]

These community schools were similar to today's charter schools but were much less regulated. Surprisingly, Texas had private school voucher and charter school systems in place in

---

113   Constitutional Convention Debates, 1875
114   Texas Constitution, Article 7 Section 1
115   Eby, The Development of Education in Texas, 1925

the late 19th and early 20th centuries. Few Texans are aware of this fact.[116]

Proponents of the Reconstruction Era, top-down, centralized, government-run system were disappointed with the *Constitution's* language, saying the community school system "destroyed districting" and played "fast and loose with the very foundation" of their preferred state controlled system.[117] But things did improve from their perspective because incorporated towns "especially after the year 1880…turned away from private schools which furnished facilities chiefly for the well-to-do, in order to establish public free schools open equally to all children."[118] However, community schools survived for decades afterwards.

This is Billy Walker's analysis: "The Community system of schools established in 1854 and continued in 1876 maximized

---

116   Parker and Weiss, "Litigating Edgewood: Constitutional Standards and Application to Educational Choice," *The Review of Litigation.* Volume 10, Number 1, 1991 UT Law Publications
117   Eby, *The Development of Education in Texas*, 1925
118   ibid

liberty by granting state support to almost unlimited parental choice and control. Modern programs for expanded educational choice, such as voucher systems, reflect a similar desire for individual or family choice unfettered by governmental control."[119]

An interesting footnote in the history of that time is that "the first president of the Texas State Teachers' Association [TSTA]…[Dr. Crane] was strongly biased in favor of the New York State plan of school organization which permitted the use of state funds for the support of private and denominational institutions of learning."[120] TSTA's first president was a private school choice proponent. However, TSTA now strongly opposes private school choice.[121]

Private schools remained a part of the public free school system in Texas for quite some time: "Some developments of minor significance appeared during these years, [circa 1907] among them the decline of private schools. The marked improvement in the character of the town schools lessened the prejudice against them, and even the wealthier people began to send their children to these rather than to the private schools."[122]

Clearly, by any reasonable analysis of their original intent, the Texas founders did intend to empower parents and communities to make decisions about the education of their students. In fact, during the 1875 constitutional debate on the issue of centralized control over education, one delegate, Mr. Sansom, said: "I do not hesitate to say that I believe there could not be

---

119   Billy Walker, Executive Director TASB, *Intent of the Framers in the Education Provisions of the Texas Constitution of 1876*, p.670
120   ibid
121   Texas State Teachers Association, TSTA statement on school vouchers, Waxahachie Daily Light (Aug. 24, 2012)
122   ibid

found a dozen members of this Convention who would affirm their belief in the existence of such power in the State."[123]

Yet today, most Texans think the original intent of our *Texas Constitution* was just the opposite.

---

123   1875 Constitutional Convention Debates

Appendix to Chapter 11

Documentation of the existence of community schools well into the 20th Century:

> "Community schools arose in Texas in opposition to a post-Civil War centralized school system."[124] Charter school type community schools were around well into the 20th Century as follows: "A school district was formed to include Fairdale by the Sabine County Commissioners Court on July 11, 1904. However, 'free community schools' were established by the state prior to that time...."[125] Old Glory, Texas and surrounding areas appear to have had community schools through the 1920s. "With consolidation of five community schools, a building was erected at Old Glory in 1930 to serve an enrollment that peaked at 280 in 1936-1937...."[126] Marlin Texas: "Marlin had private schools before the county was organized, and it was not until 1923 that public schools were available."[127] "When the course of the Galveston, Harrisburg & San Antonio Railroad, came through Cibolo and Schertz into San Antonio in 1877, it brought economic development and growth with it. During this time, children in the Green Valley, Cibolo Valley, Lower Valley and Schertz areas attended schools established under the community school system. Under the community school system, Lower Valley School was established in 1877 (closed in 1966) and Green Valley School was established in 1887

---

124 A.W. Garrett, Community Schools in 19th Century Texas
125 From a History of Fairdale, Sabine County, TX; www.toledo-bend.com:
126 xcourthouseforsale.com/history.htm, accessed 6/6/2014.
127 www.kossercafe.com/marlinhistory.html

(closed in 1955)."[128] "Before schools were formally organized, Deaf Smith County pioneers provided an education for their children in private homes. Community schools sprang up as the area developed. From 1893 through the mid-forties some fifty schools were scattered throughout the county."[129] "The first tax-supported school opened in 1880 under the name of "Bryan Grade School," and its first graduates completed the 10th Grade School four years later. Private schools joining the educational system included Allen Academy in 1899 and Villa Maria Ursuline Academy for girls in 1901."[130]

---

128 www.scuc.txed.net
129 www.texashistory.unt.edu
130 www.bryantx.gov

CHAPTER 12

Are We Funding Our Own Demise Through Higher Education?

> Men born to freedom are naturally alert to repel invasion of their liberty by evil-minded rulers. The greater dangers to liberty lurk in insidious encroachment by men of zeal, well-meaning but without understanding.
> —Justice Louis Brandeis,
> Olmstead v. United States

In late 2019 protestors in Hong Kong risked their lives and freedoms by waving the American flag and singing the United States National Anthem. Yet, professors in American colleges, who are paid by American taxpayers, consistently attack and undermine American values and re-write American history.

Is it any surprise then that much public attention has focused on political support for socialism? And this support is not unique among liberal politicians. American Millennials have a more favorable opinion of socialism than of capitalism, despite the lessons of world history and empirical evidence to the contrary. In fact, polls indicate that a majority of America's Millennials would prefer to live in socialist, fascist, or communist regimes than under capitalism.[131] Wow!

---

131 *The Washington Post*, November 4, 2017

To paraphrase Winston Churchill: The main vice of capitalism is the uneven distribution of prosperity. The main vice of socialism is the even distribution of misery.

> **For decades, professors have indoctrinated students with anti-American values. The political climate has become almost completely one-sided on most campuses.**
> —Chris Talgo, Heartland Institute

We should not blame young politicians and other Millennials for their views and ignorance of history. Americans send billions of dollars each year to institutions of higher education where left-wing professors control and dominate the agenda and who also train our new public school teachers.

Are we financing our own demise?

If more money is needed for public education, perhaps politicians should consider the financial waste of higher education and divert some funds that support it to public education. Far too many colleges and universities have become de facto propaganda factories where professors, who have little experience in the real world, sow their seeds of hatred toward free markets into young minds, who also lack real world experience. **Traditional liberal thought has been replaced with radical left-wing propaganda in many of our great institutions of higher education.**

The minds of rich trust-fund students, and those who feel disenfranchised, provide a fertile ground for such bias. Meanwhile an unwitting public, who work and thrive in a market driven system, continue to finance this very expensive higher education system, one where tuitions and other costs are growing at rates substantially higher than the rate of inflation.

Surveys indicate that young people know little about the founding of America, the founding documents, or of the philosophy that has provided the freedoms we all take for granted and that has allowed America to prosper. History has been edited, reality ignored, and the flames of hatred have been fanned—ostensibly to advance some illusive utopia with social justice without "evil" profits—a utopian fantasy unseen in the history of mankind. All the while the American public is paying the tab for this treacherous Alice in Wonderland, ivory-tower illusion. Why do we continue to permit this to happen?

To paraphrase Milton Friedman: **Most liberals are good people trying to do good.**

Our universities are dominated by social warrior professors who, although misguided, are attempting to do good. However, these professors should provide accurate, and unbiased, information regarding all political systems. History is rich with examples of all of these systems and of the contrasts between market and command economies: East Germany vs. West Germany; North Korea vs. South Korea; Cuba vs. Bahamas; U.S.A. vs. USSR; etc. Without an accurate understanding of history, we are doomed to repeat the failures of history. Given an unbiased presentation, the youth of America will exercise wisdom and determine the right direction for their futures. Truth will prevail when provided.

U.S. Rep. Alexandria Ocasio Cortez said in one interview that capitalism has not always existed. Although that might be debatable, the concept of freedom has always existed. The term capitalism was coined in the mid-1800s by Karl Marx, but a much better term for "capitalism" is "free enterprise." Capitalism (free markets) is the very essence of freedom. Economic freedom is a natural right: The right to work where you wish, to freely choose how and what you spend your earnings on, the right to sell your services, and the freedom to own property. In other words, the pursuit of happiness.

What today's socialists fail to comprehend is that freedom, and the societal wellbeing which liberty creates, cannot endure without free markets. Freedom cannot flourish without the right to fail and the opportunity to succeed. The allocation of goods and services can only be allocated in one of two manners—by markets or by command. With command comes tyranny, whereas freedom can only exist with markets. Freedom cannot survive without the prospect of profit and the profit motive—the pursuit of happiness.

Today's socialist fail to comprehend that freedom cannot survive without free markets.

Few liberal professors have experienced success in the real world. Most do not fully comprehend the nature of profits. **The word "profit" is probably one of the most misunderstood words in our vocabulary.** Profit is not evil. Profit is simply a financial or personal benefit. You might profit by changing jobs. You might profit by attaining a college degree. Each paycheck you receive represents the profit you earn by working instead of staying at home. The freedom to profit is an essential element of economic freedom.

Profit does not necessarily mean money. One might profit spiritually by attending church or reading scripture. One might profit morally by contributing to charity.

The freedom to choose how to spend your time, purchase what you wish with your earnings, travel where you want, and determine what you wish to produce through your trade or profession, these are the bases of a market economy. Freedom to choose is what makes markets. Markets are critical to assuring liberty. Just ask an immigrant who has actually lived in a command economy.

A socialist government, which controls or owns the means of production, inherently restricts individual freedom. **If government denies someone the right to sell you something, it therefore is also prohibiting you from buying that item.** Limiting one side of the economic freedom equation inevitably restricts the other side as well.

A core economic freedom is simply the ability to profit from your work, which includes profiting from your savings. If you save, you might turn those savings into capital investments. Your car is a capital investment, which you may drive to work. A carpenter's hammer is a capital investment. A kid with a lawnmower can profit from his labor, and from his investment in a lawnmower by mowing lawns.

Absent a profit motive, a society will not foster innovation generated by a free society. Otherwise, why would the Chinese be stealing our intellectual property today? The Chinese people are brilliant, creative, wise; however, individual freedom (and therefore, the profit motive) is greatly restricted in China. The freedom to profit and innovate is exactly the reason the United States defeated the USSR in the Cold War.

Little innovation comes from command economies. Does anyone actually believe that, if government ran the telephone company, or even if the telephone industry were currently as highly regulated as it was during most of the 20th century, that we would have smart phones today? We all know the answer to that question.

Free enterprise has resulted in greater social justice than any command economy in the world.

The profit motive results in greater innovation and productivity than any command economy can. Free enterprise has, therefore, resulted in greater social justice than any other system in history—just look at the evidence. The rich or middle classes in many countries would gladly trade places with America's poor—many people around the world have risked their lives in attempts to do so.

To update and build upon an editorial by Professor Thomas Sowell from several decades ago: Steve Jobs delivered more music to the masses than Beethoven; it was not the enlightened professors who brought light to the masses, it was Thomas Edison; it is not government bureaucrats who make sure the merchandise we want is readily available, it's places like Costco, Wal-Mart, Amazon, and millions of small businesses. These establishments would not exist absent the profit motive.

Markets deliver goods and services to us economically and efficiently without the shortages and surpluses inherently found in command economies. Without the profit motive, this huge benefit to society would not exist. Without the profit motive, millions have starved in command economies. That is not social justice.

Good people trying to do good can often inadvertently do more harm than good. Even the early American settlers learned firsthand the failures of socialism. William Bradford and his followers were trying to do good when the Pilgrims experimented with socialism back in the 1620s. They implemented communal farms in Plymouth, Massachusetts, three centuries before the USSR tried the same failed policy. In every instance where socialism has been tried, it has been a huge failure. In these systems, few have an incentive to work hard because there is no reward for personal effort and hard work.

Good people trying to do good often inadvertently do more harm than good.

The absence of freedom, and therefore the profit motive, is exactly why the Soviets lost the Cold War. That is also the reason that three centuries earlier, lack of productivity resulted in famine in the communal Pilgrim farms, and the Pilgrims abandoned the first American experiment with socialism. Many people believe that the first Thanksgiving was actually a celebration of capitalism, as the Pilgrims flourished once abandoning the failed concept of communal sharing of land and the communal sharing of the fruits of their production and labor.

Much of today's curricula overlook this critical chapter in American history. Misguided, but well-meaning, progressive professors instead seek what they view as social justice. Of that mindset Dinesh D'Souza says, "The ingenuity of modern progressivism is that it produces nothing, but stakes a moral claim to the wealth produced by others in the name of 'social justice.'" **Those misguided professors simply overlook the fact that that kind of social justice was attempted back in the 1600s here in America**, and that it has failed to produce social justice when tried thereafter around the world.

Freedom and free markets have provided greater social justice than any system throughout the history of mankind. That is true even though autocratic rule, and the abandonment of freedom and markets, has usually been imposed in the name of social justice.

In an effort to take the same moral high road, many Millennials express a desire to work in the non-profit arena. What they fail to realize, and are not told by their left-wing professors, is that no enterprise is actually non-profit, as someone invariably profits from the endeavors of the institution. Someone earns a profit in the form of a paycheck.

In reality there is no such thing as a non-profit. Instead these are tax-exempt organizations; therefore, the "non-profit" label is actually only a tax classification. That is not to say that "non-profits" are not doing good work. Many definitely are. The point is that, in almost every endeavor, someone profits.

Colleges and universities are tax-exempt institutions; however, professors take home handsome profits in the form of paychecks for limited hours actually worked. These paychecks are paid or subsidized by taxpayers, most of whom earn their livelihoods in the marketplace of freedom—the very system that is being undermined daily while ordinary citizens foot the bill.

Yes, we are funding our own demise.

ACKNOWLEDGEMENTS

The author hereby expresses a special thanks to all those who helped provide editorial advice and feedback on this book including:

My wife **Elise Grusendorf** for her patience and ongoing editorial help;

Dr. Byron Schlomach for his detailed and helpful review of the initial draft;

Doug Rogers for his professional guidance, based on his years as leader of ATPE, and for his professional expertise;

Dr. Don McAdams for his insight and help based on his many years of leadership in the education community;

Dr. John Merrifield for his review, guidance, and editorial comments;

Melissa Martin for her insight and perspective as a practicing classroom teacher;

Jim Windham for his help and feedback based on his many years of experience in the education reform arena;

Dr. Rod Page, former U.S. Secretary of Education, for his insight and review;

Linda Pavlik for her review and insight;

Dr. Kenneth Poppe, a former ATPE teacher of the year, for his insight and help;

Adam Robinson for graphic design and layout of the book, and to;

Mom, **Ruby Lois Grusendorf [1917-2009]**, who told me on more than one occasion to get a good education because: *"That is the only thing that they can never take away from you."*

ABOUT THE AUTHOR

Kent Grusendorf was elected to the Texas State Board of Education in 1982. Four years later he was elected to the Texas Legislature where he served for 20 years. In both political races he defeated an incumbent by running primarily on the issue of education reform. Once elected to the Texas House of Representatives, Speaker Gib Lewis appointed him to the House Public Education Committee, to the Legislative Education Board, and with consent of Governor Bill Clements, to the Governor's Select Committee tasked to deal with the state's very first court finding that the school finance system was unconstitutional: Edgewood I. He has been involved in each round of school finance litigation thereafter.

Grusendorf served on numerous other select committees over the years and served as chairman of the 29 member House Select Committee on School Finance, which was tasked to deal with the *West Orange* school finance decision in 2003. He also served on the Southern Regional Education Board's Executive Committee, and served as chairman of the American Legislative Exchange Conference (ALEC) Education Task Force. During his last two sessions in the legislature, 2003 and 2005, he chaired the House Public Education Committee.

Grusendorf has authored hundreds of articles on education that have been published in the Wall Street Journal, Dallas Morning News, Fort Worth Star Telegram, Austin American Statesman, Houston Chronicle, San Antonio Express News, Texas Tribune, Quorum Report, and many other publications over the years.